SINGLE ME

Learning to Love the Unwanted Path of Singleness

NERI MORRIS

NM//

NERI MORRIS.

Single Me: Learning to Love the Unwanted Path of Singleness

Copyright © Neridah Morris, 2020

First published 2020

Published by Neridah Morris

Email: hello@nerimorris.com

Web: www.nerimorris.com

All rights reserved. Without limiting the rights under copyright reserved above, no part of this publication may be reproduced, stored in or introduced into a database and retrieval system or transmitted in any form or any means (electronic, mechanical, photocopying, recording or otherwise) without the prior written permission of both the owner of copyright and the above publishers.

All Scripture quotations, unless otherwise indicated, are taken from the Holy Bible, New International Version®, NIV®. Copyright ©1973, 1978, 1984, 2011 by Biblica, Inc.™ Used by permission of Zondervan. All rights reserved worldwide. www.zondervan.com. The "NIV" and "New International Version" are trademarks registered in the United States Patent and Trademark Office by Biblica, Inc.™

Cover art by Rusyn Viktoriia

Single Me

Neridah Morris

ISBN 978-0-6489764-1-7

Contents

1. Who is Single Me?   1

Part One
The Reality of Single Me

1. You Are Allowed to Feel What You Feel   17
2. Lonely   25
3. Rejected   33
4. Forgotten   41
5. Confused   53
6. Jealous   65

Part Two
The Context of Single Me

7. Not Everything Given to You Is Useful for You   73
8. Do Me a Favour; Don't Do Me a Favour   83
9. The Debate of a Soul Mate   91
10. The Idol of Marriage   99

Part Three
The Truth of Single Me

11. Just When You Thought You Were Off the Hook, Single One   107
12. Welcoming Growth   115
13. Redefining Success   129
14. Challenging Fear   135
15. Realigning Expectations   141

Part Four
The Beauty of Single Me

16. Freedom   151
17. Contentment   157
18. Gratitude   165

19. Endurance	173
20. Surrender	179
Notes	187
Acknowledgements	189
About the Author	193

ONE

Who is Single Me?

I didn't want to write this book. Partly because it seemed like a daunting task and partly because I didn't want to become known as 'that single girl who wrote that book'. Which is a huge assumption, because there is no guarantee anyone but my mum is going to read this.

Back in 2018, I unexpectedly found myself at the opening night of Hillsong Conference in Sydney. I had returned from America only the day before, and a friend offered me her ticket for the opening night. Thinking I could stave off jetlag, I opted to go along. I had no real expectations for the evening. It had been a while since I'd gone to a Hillsong event, and I wasn't out to receive a word from God or to have him radically move in my life. I was just trying to stay awake!

However, I would soon discover that God had other plans. In the middle of worship, I had a little conversation within myself, prompted by the Holy Spirit.

It began with that dangerous prayer: 'Lord, use me; I'll do whatever you want.'

And I felt a response within my spirit surface. 'It's time to write the book.'

'What book?' I asked.

'You know what book.' Came the reply.

And immediately, dread filled me. 'I don't want to write a book on singleness. I don't want to become known as that "single girl".' I promptly put the conversation to the side and just enjoyed the music. But like a pesky fly, the words of the Holy Spirit kept buzzing around in my head.

I didn't want to do it, but I couldn't ignore the call.

I picked up my laptop a few days later, not knowing a thing about writing, how to structure a book or even what I wanted to say. And I just wrote. I started with my story. More specifically, I started writing about the failed relationships and the lessons I had learnt from them. Which was a weird place to start, thinking back on it now, because this was meant to be a book on singleness – and I was writing about relationships. But it was where I needed to start.

I got to 6,000 words when I met a guy. 'Well, maybe I was just meant to *start* the book,' I thought, and promptly put my writing project down.

God, as always, had other plans. The relationship I was pursuing with this guy ended six months later, and I found myself in Melbourne – disillusioned, a bit broken, angry and very, very single.

I started to write again. There was no better time to write a book on singleness than when I was feeling my most single. By the time I flew home from those couple of weeks in Melbourne, I had written over 25,000 words.

That time showed me that what I wanted to write most was a book I'd want to read in my current situation. I never wanted to be single in my thirties, but I am. I know I'm not alone in this. There are many single Christians out there who find themselves partnerless, not necessarily by choice, and not for want of trying or for lack of praying. For some reason, being married in our twenties was simply not the journey for us.

After the dissolving of that six-month relationship, I set out to find some guidance, something to help make sense of all of this. I didn't want to hear all the ways I needed to get out of being single; I didn't want to hear the Christian clichés or Sunday school answers. I just wanted to know that I wasn't alone in being single and that there was hope. I wanted to understand why singleness has been such a dominant theme in my story.

I have read quite a few books over the years that provide advice on how to find your spouse, what to do while waiting for your spouse, how to date and so on. But there is very little out there that looks at singleness as a season to embrace. The message of most books on singleness is communicated through the lens of getting out of singleness, not learning to love it as it is. In all my reading, I found nothing that was really helpful in providing a framework that would help me not resent my singleness.

By the time I reached my thirties, faced with the stark truth that being single was still part of my reality, I was tired. I was tired of reading all those books – books whose language made me feel inadequate and whose advice didn't lead to the right outcome, even though I'd followed it all. I was tired of being told I was too this and not enough that. Maybe I should do more of this and a little less of that. I had advice fatigue and was riddled with disillusionment about the whole marriage thing. I knew what I wanted, but felt like I'd somehow missed the 'soul mate allocation day' when God was handing them out. If I'm honest, it still feels a little impossible.

I remember reflecting on my age and lack of spouse and thinking, 'Well, if God has me single in my thirties, then maybe I should figure out what he has for me in this instead of fighting it.' It wasn't a Damascus Road experience, but it was a defining statement and one I have been reflecting on since. Truthfully, it has helped me find what is good about being single.

This change in focus from what I don't have to what God has for me right here, in this season, has led to this book. It made me realise that maybe I wasn't the only person who felt this way. Maybe I wasn't the only one frustrated with the type of support out there for single Christians in their thirties. Maybe I wasn't the only one who was trying to hold the tension of the now and not yet. I am no expert on this journey, but I'm a willing running partner.

Before I share more about what kind of book this is and invite you into its pages, you probably want to know a bit more about my story and why singleness has been an unexpectedly dominant topic.

Looking for a love story

It was a typical early summer evening in Australia. Warm, clear and beautiful. The fragrances of summer drifted past my friend and I as we walked along the footpath, taking in the Christmas lights and allowing the magic they created to fill us with a sense of awe and wonder.

Our conversation naturally drifted to plans over Christmas. Living on the North Shore of Sydney, I would be heading to the mountains where my family lived to spend Christmas with them. I was really looking forward to some time off after Christmas from my part time job and online retail business. My friend asked me what my plans were for that time, and I told her I didn't have any. Maybe I'd just go to the beach, see who was around to grab a coffee with. It was going to be low key.

Suddenly feeling uncomfortable that my Christmas break was shaping up to be so boring and not wanting to dwell on it, I shifted the conversation her way, asking what her plans were. They were to have Christmas with her family, and then she, her husband and their little boy would be going away with two other families from church to spend a few days by the water, making the most of the fact that one of the couples had a boat.

My old friend jealousy began to swell in the pit of my stomach. The break sounded amazing and well-deserved for everyone going. But, like a bruise being pressed on, I felt the pain of being single spreading its ache through me. I fought hard to ignore it, to push it out of my awareness. But the ache didn't leave. It just sat there, a constant reminder for the rest of our walk. Externally, nothing had changed. My friend and I finished our Christmas light gazing and said our goodbyes, and I drove off. But internally, the pain was there, present and palpable, reminding me of what I didn't have.

I deeply wanted to go on that trip. In fact, it wasn't even the trip itself that I wanted. It was that I wanted to at least *qualify* for the trip. I wanted a husband and family to share Christmas with. I wanted to have plans with other couples for the post-Christmas break. I wanted to be able to say, 'Me, Bob and the kids are heading north for a week'. At thirty-five, I wanted to have a tribe. I wanted to feel tethered to something. I wanted to feel like I had a home.

I had a vision for what my life should look like by this point, and to be honest, hanging alone for the Christmas holidays wasn't part of the script.

After all, I was *supposed* to be married with kids by now.

I can't remember how young it started, this obsession with happily ever after. I feel like I've been hardwired this way from birth. Even as a small kid, my little heart loved love stories. I was captivated by Disney classics like *The Little Mermaid* and *Beauty and the Beast*. I wanted a love story of my own. You know the narrative – the one where the boy sees you from across the room and is mesmerised by your beauty. He begins to make his way towards you as you meet his gaze, becoming lost in his compelling eyes that seem to beckon you to draw closer. And as you meet in the middle of the dance floor (because that's where all great love stories start) he says something captivating like 'I saw you from across the room and I thought you were so stunningly beautiful that I just had to find out who you were.' You smile coyly as he takes you in his arms and spins you around the dancefloor. And as you begin to slow-dance, you both realise that you've found it. You have found 'The One'. Your soul mate. The person you are meant to be with for the rest of your life.

This was what my little heart hoped for and dreamt about. Maybe not that exact scenario, but something where I would be noticed and pursued. I wanted a moment where the whole world changed because I had found someone who wanted me.

And just occasionally, I had a taste of it. My family used to go on vacation to the same caravan park every year. It is in a beautiful, somewhat untouched part of the world, nestled on the south coast of New South Wales. My three siblings and I would spend our days riding bikes, building forts, swimming and playing. Some of my best childhood memories happened in that place.

One day by the pool, a girl I had seen around the caravan park came up to me and said, 'My brother thinks you're cute and wants to know if you want to go out with him?'

I realised that this was my moment. He had seen me from across the pool and had enough courage to send his sister as a go-between. Despite having no idea who he was or where he was in the pool, I announced, 'Yes, I will!' then dived into the pool for dramatic effect.

End scene.

Or rather, I came up for air and suddenly realised that I didn't know the name of the boy I was apparently now in a relationship with – or even what he looked like.

But I nailed the dive, so at least that part was good.

I don't really remember at what point, or how, I found out Luke's name, but I was definitely happy when I finally met my 'boyfriend' and discovered he was good-looking.

So, Luke and I were dating, but as ten-year-olds that doesn't really mean anything. From what I can remember, it consisted of hovering near each other. We didn't really talk, we never held hands, and we only ever hung out in a group.

But none of that mattered to me, because we were *boyfriend and girlfriend*. I remember writing pages and pages in my trusty diary – one of those sorts that had a padlock and key and smelt like strawberries – confessing my undying love for Luke. Despite not knowing Luke at all, other than the fact that he rode a pee-wee motorbike (how cool was my boyfriend?!), my diary entries insisted that he was the best boyfriend ever. I was sooooooo in love.

Of course, our love ended when summer did.

I'd like to blame old mate Disney for my skewed view of romance and my belief that love and marriage of epic proportions was guaranteed to me, but that would be unfair. My faith has also played a part. When I was teenager, the 'I Kissed Dating Goodbye' and purity ring movements were at their height. I read book after book about dating and love and God's plan for it all. I lapped it up, so eager to follow the path that would lead me to my husband. I had it all mapped out: get married around twenty-two, have some kids – maybe four, because I know how fun it can be to come from a big family – then around thirty, build a career. This was truly how I believed my life would play out. So, I did as the Bible (and all those books) instructed and presented my requests to God, then sat back to watch it unfold.

It was a reasonable plan. It was a solid plan. It seemed completely possible. At least, *I* thought it was. Apparently, God did not agree with my way of thinking. Instead, he has allowed the unthinkable to become my reality. I distinctly remember saying to God that to be single when I turn thirty would be a fate worse than death. Yet somehow here I am, single, childless and still trying to build a career.

I guess one out of three ain't bad.

In need of course correction

Was I wrong to think that I could be married by twenty-two? Not at all. Am I wrong to hope for marriage and children? Absolutely not. But what I have come to learn is that who you listen to matters. Defining my journey by what I saw on TV or read in some popular books was an error on my part. It led to deep disillusionment, frustration, a lot of tears, bad decisions and, ultimately, resentment towards singleness.

Obviously, I've had to do a bit of course-correction – some of which has happened in the process of writing this book! Here are some of the things I've discovered.

1. I've learnt to ask the right questions

When your life doesn't unfold in the way you expect – especially when that expectation is bound up with faith in a good God – you start to ask some questions. Like 'Why?' and 'When, God?' or 'How long until…?'

But these questions are not the right ones. Because when you're trying to come to terms with your current single status, it's not about 'why' or 'when' or 'how long'. It's about 'what' and 'who'.

What is this single thing?

Who am I, as a Christian single?

Who is single me?

All other questions focus our attention on the future, which is not always a bad thing, but it does keep us from truly experiencing the present – this moment, right here, right now. These questions keep us from embracing the now. From embracing our singleness.

I have wrestled for many years with a deep desire to be married and a reality that did not match this desire. I have fought God, fasted, prayed, pleaded, fasted again, given up, asked for forgiveness for my unbelief, gotten angry and started the whole cycle again. But through the wrestle comes revelation. Each time I have allowed myself to be real and raw with God, I have found no answer to my 'why/when/how long' questions; rather, I have found the consistent, never-changing truth that God loves me and is to be trusted. He promises good to me. He promises there is purpose in this unwanted path of singleness I find myself on. And I am too eager to see his plan unfold to walk away. (At least, that's how I feel today!)

2. I'm getting to know God's part in it all

Along with getting to know myself better in this single phase through asking the right sorts of questions, I've also been getting to know God better.

Towards the end of my twenties, I started to ask questions about what made God answer our prayers. Yes, that's how I saw it – that we 'made' God answer. If I said the right combination of words or did the right things or behaved the right way, that this would be what got a response from God, as if he were some ATM that I just needed the right PIN for. I believed he answered those he loved, and that his love needed to be earned.

Everything I thought I knew about God and about how he answers prayer, I essentially threw out the window when I entered my thirties. I hit reset. I removed the expectations of a specific answer to a specific question and instead thought that if God had me single in my thirties, then my time was better spent seeking out what he wanted me to learn or understand about myself and my situation. Everything I had tried up until that point hadn't worked, so I really had nothing to lose by hitting reset.

3. I'm finding the fruit

Believe it or not, this reset has actually been the most fruitful approach.

As I write this book, I am still single. For some readers, it may seem as though this approach therefore bears no fruit at all. But the fruit I'm talking about is not found in getting 'the desire of my heart'. The fruit is found in how God has broken down the poor theology I possessed, deconstructed my faith and rebuilt it in a way that has me more confident in his love for me.

God has taught me so much through singleness. I have learnt singleness isn't easy. I have learnt that it's hard when it feels like everyone else's lives are progressing and yours appears not to be. I have learnt that more often than not, God's answer to any question is 'Trust me', and it's my choice to do so.

I have also learnt there is a lot that is wrong with the way we view singleness within the church. I have seen the detrimental effects of exclusion because of someone's singleness due to sexual preference or a broken marriage, regardless of how much that individual loves God. I have received (and, let's face it, given as well) some terrible advice about how to deal with being single and being a Christian. I have seen once strong Christians who were diligently following the advice given to them by their church leaders about waiting for a spouse, give up and walk away because God did not meet their desire when they had expected him to.

Back to what's in this book

Some people will call this book a memoir. I guess to some extent it is. But I see it more as a collection of stories that have crafted and shaped my understanding of singleness as I've grappled with asking the right questions, getting to know God all over again and finding the fruit.

It's also not a 'how-to' book. I don't have all the answers, and I'm not out to tell you how to get out of being single. In fact, I now believe singleness is not something to 'get out of', but is a season to be embraced. My hope is to encourage, inspire or bring a small ray of hope to the people who, like me, have walked what could be considered the road less travelled in Christian circles.

This book is designed to challenge and encourage. It's designed to stimulate conversation. It's designed to get us thinking about things that we have just accepted growing up in the church. It's a book designed to help us, as Christians, better love those who are not married.

It's a book designed to say to you, dear single Christian in your thirties (or at any age), that I get it. I get the struggle. I get how hard it is.

Through my journey so far in the world of singleness, I have come to the conclusion that there are four distinct aspects of this singleness journey. The first is our current reality, how we feel, what we're experiencing on a consistent basis and how that makes this journey hard. The second is the culture we exist in, the different perspectives and opinions that surround us and the way those things can keep us second-guessing ourselves. The third is the personal work to be done. Our singleness is a unique season, but how we engage with it is entirely dependent on us. The final part is the discovery of what makes this time worth loving. And there is a lot to love about this path we did not choose. I've therefore written this book in four parts, The Reality of Single Me, The Context of Single Me, The Truth of Single Me and The Beauty of Single Me, reflecting these four different angles from which we approach singleness.

I share a lot of my journey of learning to love this unwanted path through my personal story. As I share these open and vulnerable stories, I do need to add a disclaimer. These are *my memories* of these stories. The people mentioned in them have had their names changed, and I have altered some of the details slightly to protect them. Without a doubt, these people will have a different interpretation of how things unfolded. We experience life from different perspectives, different belief systems, different upbringings, different childhood wounds. We are all always working through something. So please read this with the understanding that this is my experience, my perspective, my thoughts and my lessons of this journey.

My hope and prayer is that you will laugh with me, commiserate with me, nod in agreement with some of the things I've experienced and ultimately join me in changing the way we relate to ourselves, finding a sense of satisfaction in our season of singleness and learning to truly embrace 'single me'.

The Reality of Single Me

ONE

You Are Allowed to Feel What You Feel

It is Saturday morning. I always opt for a lazy Saturday morning in bed (sometimes Sunday too), choosing to teeter for as long as possible in that delicious half-asleep, half-awake state, where time is suspended and the to-do list for the day has not yet risen to consciousness.

Curling my hands around my coffee cup, I pick up my phone and hit the big bright blue button with the white 'F' in the middle (because starting your day with Facebook is true wisdom). Immediately I am thrust into despair as I see a friend of mine proudly sporting a beautiful ring on her left hand and some cheesy caption like 'Does this ring make me look engaged??? #livingmybestlife' or 'Today's forecast is shiny with a 100% chance of MARRIAGE!!! #yeahhedid #idoboo'.

A flashback to last night's binge session of *Gossip Girl* starts to play in my head, just as my stomach gurgles to remind me of the entire tub of ice cream I consumed. I pull the blankets up over my head, trying to bury the memory, and ponder the thought of selling everything I own and running away to live the simple life with some Tibetan monks.

Being single is crap.

Okay, maybe that's just a little dramatic, but I've had these Bridget Jones moments more often that I'd like to admit. Social media has many wonderful attributes. Filtering posts and stories that remind me of how single I am is not one of them.

The single season is a constant battle. You want to be joyful for your friends as they transition into married life or start a family. But while you're outwardly cheering them on, inwardly you are trying to pull yourself out of a pit of despair at how single you feel, all the while doing it with a smile. It's hard. It's tough. It's lonely.

You can feel as though you are marooned on an island watching everyone else escape on rafts made out of palm leaves and spit, and you can't quite figure out how on earth they did it. (Where the heck is MacGyver when you need him?) I mean, you have all the tools … why can't you get it together?!

I've found being single is a journey filled with so much uncertainty and confusion. It's a constant state of tension, wanting marriage and trying to be proactive about it, while living in the reality of yet again waking up next to no one.

Over the years I have watched many friends struggle with wanting to find someone. Some have been successful in this pursuit with seemingly little effort. Others have thrown everything at it – read all the books, been to all the seminars, signed up to various online dating sites, done the blind date thing, tried everything they can think of – and still remain single.

I have also witnessed friends who have honestly and earnestly sought the Lord, trying really hard to be patient, but to no avail. Ultimately, they feel as though they have been forgotten. God has let them down. So, they walk away from God and his church in search of greener pastures.

As Christians struggling with singleness, I believe we want to trust God. Trust he has a plan for us. Trust that he knows our desires. Trust he cares about these desires. Trust in his goodness and kindness. But when relationship after relationship fails and the biological clock keeps ticking, it gets harder and harder to trust the character of God with the dreams and desires we hold.

The shame of it all

One of the toughest things about being a single Christian – and, I believe, one of the reasons we so rarely talk about it – is the shame that is frequently associated with singleness. There is a deep sense of shame that hovers over our relationship status because we feel as though we're not good enough on our own. Or we fear our singleness means we are unlovable, rejected, not wanted. Feeling unlovable keeps us in a cycle of shame and despair. And when this narrative of shame and rejection plays on loop, it keeps us from what we long for the most – deep connection.

Connection. It's what every human on earth craves: to be seen and known and accepted. As Brené Brown says: 'Connection is why we're here; it is what gives purpose and meaning to our lives.'[1]

Harvard University conducted a study of 268 male graduates in which they monitored participants' lives for 75 years in order to find out what made for a happy and fulfilling life. Taking data samples at regular intervals, the researchers came to understand a great deal about the contributions of work, money and success. But the main contributor to a fulfilling life? Connection. As a Huffington Post writer pithily summed it up, 'the conclusion of the study, not in a medical but in a psychological sense, is that connection is the whole shooting match.'[2]

Connection. That's it. That is what life is about. That is the end game.

We all want to feel as though someone knows us, the whole of us, and loves us regardless of what they find. And not just loves us, but is committed to continuing to be there despite the external pressures that unfold or the mistakes we make. That thought is scary to some people because it means that even the parts of themselves they do not love will need to be revealed if deep connection is to be achieved. But the desire, the need, for deep connection remains.

Yet somehow, many of us who are single feel shame, not only about being single in the first place, but about wanting connection. It seems that if we admit we want something different and actively pursue it, we may get branded desperate.

Longing for connection

I had a friend in my twenties who was constantly going on dates. She would talk a lot about how she just wanted to be married. It was a deep desire of hers, and at times I'll admit I judged her as 'a bit desperate', which probably stemmed more from jealousy. I marvelled at her confidence to get out there and date as many guys as possible, something I didn't really do because I felt I'd be setting myself up for immediate rejection.

But judging my friend as 'desperate' was so wrong. She was actually displaying a very normal, very real, very natural desire for deep connection. She craved to be seen and known. It's the exact same desire I had. The exact same desire you have. The exact same desire we all have.

So why do we judge people's expression of that desire? Is it because we see in them the very thing we desire and are too fearful to own it and express it in a healthy way? This was my experience. I judged her because I wanted to have the confidence she had in going out to pursue her desires, but felt like that was so beyond me due to my fear of rejection. So rather than acknowledge that and work on myself, I cast judgement on her – and on my own desire for connection.

As I've grown more confident and put myself out there more, I've had the tables turned on me more than once. Just the other week, I was having a drink with a friend and was sharing with her my recent experiences in the world of relationships and a bunch of revelations about how I was going about finding a partner. In the course of our conversation she showed me a picture of someone who was attending an event she was going to. I commented on how good looking the guy was and started wondering out loud how could I score an invite to this event.

She responded by saying, 'Well, you seem to really want a relationship right now.'

I felt completely judged in that moment. Whatever my friend's intention with her comment, it made me feel that my desire for deep connection was a bad thing, something to be ashamed of, something that should remain unexpressed.

It seems that if we don't put on a brave face and show ourselves to be completely content with where God has us, we are judged. Maybe you won't say it to me directly, but within your heart or mind you have branded me as someone whose sole purpose is to find a spouse. You've heard the whisperings.

'She's a bit desperate…'

'She is always on the hunt… all she talks about is guys…'

'She just doesn't seem to be able to be content with Christ ... how sad...'

It's the double-edged sword of shame. On the one hand, singleness is judged as defective. On the other, desiring a relationship is judged as distasteful or desperate. As single women, we run from being labelled a 'spinster' or 'old maid' or any other such disempowering names, while equally trying to run from being branded a desperate, guy-obsessed woman! We are not satisfied in our singleness, yet we are expected to be. We are expected to not complain, whinge or whine about the lack of quality options out there or how annoying it is that yet another date didn't go anywhere, all because we fear judgement from those around us.

But this approach is disempowering, degrading and ultimately not God-glorifying, because all human beings have the same desire for deep connection. I'll repeat that: *we all have the same desire for deep connection.*

'A deep sense of love and belonging is an irreducible need of all people. We are biologically, cognitively, physically, and spiritually wired to love, to be loved, and to belong,' says Brené Brown.

Yet we read about this deep connection in the millions of books out there about marriage. But there is little out there that discusses what healthy connection could look like for single people. There is little formal research around this concept and singleness, especially within the Christian context. What research has been conducted (mainly in America and Europe) points to the 'anecdotal evidence [that] many single Christians – be they never married, divorced or widowed – struggle with feelings of isolation, marginalisation, disappointment and even invisibility within their church communities.'[3]

We see this in the numerous marriage and parenting courses available, designed to serve and equip those who are married and have children. But where are the courses for those who are single that aren't just about how to *get out of* being single?

I feel it's time to bring that which is in the dark – those things that make us feel shame around singleness and longing for connection – into the light. There needs to be amplification of the conversations that have begun, alongside greater awareness. The only way forward is to raise the volume of the conversation, for single people to speak up and for the church community to acknowledge and engage with singleness, not through the lens of marriage, but through its own lens. One that rightly shows singleness for all it is, not what it is not.

Bring it into the light

'Only when we are brave enough to explore the darkness will we discover the infinite power of our light,' says Brené Brown. The exploration of darkness, of the things we feel shame over, allows us to diffuse and remove the power this has over us. As I have learnt to embrace the negative feelings I hold over singleness and brought them into the light, I have empowered myself to move past them. This is what I want for you – for us. I want to bring that which is shrouded in darkness and shame into the light so that we can step into the power found there.

In this darkness we feel confused. We feel lonely. We feel rejected. We feel forgotten, as though no one understands. We feel jealous, which leads to despair and sadness.

So, I want to talk about it. I want to talk about the feelings common to singleness. I want to bring them into the light. I want to bring them into the light not by listing ten things you can do to lift yourself out of the funk, or my top tips on getting the partner of your dreams. I don't even want to talk about it in a way that is full of Sunday school answers and shallow Christian responses – because you deserve better. You deserve more than just a 'chin-up Charlie' response to the very real, very deep feelings you have because you crave to be fully seen and fully known.

I want to be real. I want to be honest. I want to be open. If we're going to change the dialogue about singleness for Christians, then it has to start with honesty. It has to start with taking a good, hard look at what we feel and not being ashamed of the dark moments in this journey. It's going to take the courage to step out of the darkness and into the light.

TWO

Lonely
_____

I attended a friend's wedding a few weeks after my boyfriend of almost a year had broken up with me. He was supposed to join me at this wedding, but due to the break-up, I was attending this wedding on my own.

It is a truly horrible feeling to have to admit to the bride your 'plus one' is now a minus.

With the break-up still very, very fresh, I did my best to put on a brave face. I mustered every ounce of courage I had to stand up in front of everyone and say a prayer for my friends during their ceremony. I kept it together when asked to hold my friends' drinks and handbags as they took photos in front of the harbour with their respective others. I even managed to make small talk when the conversation swung to babies or a friend's recent engagement.

But a simple chair was my undoing.

Arriving at the buzzing reception, my friends and I eagerly hunted down our table, scanning the little cards for our names. Walking the full length of the table, my eyes came across my name. I was seated in the last chair, at the end of the table. Someone was seated to my left ... but no one to my right. In that moment, a deep, dark pit of despair opened up inside of me. I felt as though I wanted to curl up and die. Not because I was angry for being seated at the end of the table, but because I realised that if my boyfriend and I were still together, I wouldn't be sitting at the end of the table, alone.

There would have been a seat to my right where he would have sat. We would have laughed and talked and maybe even awkwardly shuffled on the dance floor together, ending the night with his arms around me as we waved farewell to the happy couple.

Instead, there was only one chair. A married couple sat to my left. Married couples were seated directly across from me.

And I felt so alone.

The 'verb' of loneliness

Loneliness is a horrible feeling.

It feels icky, uncomfortable and worst of all, inescapable. It has a nasty habit of following you wherever you go. When loneliness is present, rooms full of people feel just as isolating as a cave in the wilderness. It's a feeling no one wants to sit in for long.

In fact, it is a feeling that physically propels us to act. We take physical action to remove the uncomfortable emotion we are experiencing. We don't want to be alone, so when we feel it, we reach for a way out of it. This could look like escaping through bingeing on Netflix. It could look like filling up our schedules with coffees and dinners with friends with no space to actually be alone. It could look like reaching for something, anything, to make the lonely feelings go away, even for a short while. Because we are hardwired for connection, when we do feel lonely, we seek to find connection again, to return to our true state.

In that moment, with the chair, I physically had to escape, and I couldn't leave the venue since the reception had just started. So, I did the next best thing. I politely excused myself and made a beeline for the bathroom. Locked in a stall, I could release at least a few of the tears I had been holding back all day. Every moment that had pointed to love and marriage in the ceremony served only to highlight my lack of it. This pain had compounded throughout the day, and I felt as though the weight of the deep rejection and loneliness I was experiencing was going to crush me.

I cried silently in the stall, letting the weight of loneliness release a little – at least enough to feel like I could breathe again. After a few moments, I pulled myself together. Not wanting my friends to come looking for me, I checked my face in the mirror, hoping they wouldn't notice my watery eyes, and made my way back to that seat.

The feeling was still very much there; I had just managed to stuff it far enough back into its box to somewhat enjoy the evening, despite feeling desperately alone in a room full of people.

Reflecting back on this event, a few questions come to mind. Why didn't I tell anyone? Why didn't I reach out? Why didn't I speak up about how I was feeling?

Recent studies have shown that loneliness is just as bad for our health as smoking. The isolation can contribute to an early death. And this isn't only applicable to people who are isolated or choose to isolate themselves. That night at the wedding, in a room of around 120 people, I felt desperately lonely. And yet, I chose to not tell anyone. I had many good friends there that night who would have understood and supported me, but I chose to not let anyone in on my pain. I chose not to reach out.

The more I thought about it, the more I realised it was because I was embarrassed. I didn't want people's pity.

'Poor Neri… she must feel so lonely…'

'It's okay hon, God has a plan… '

I didn't want people to think they had to wrap me up in cotton wool. I didn't want their pity, and I didn't want their platitudes.

I just didn't want to feel lonely anymore.

Is loneliness a sin?

I spend most of my week in a co-working space, which proves incredibly helpful when needing to seek out other opinions or thoughts about anything from the best place on the street to get food through to deep theological questions. In fact, the latter is my favourite part about working in a co-working space that exists within a church. I'm surrounded by some very smart, very well read, very passionate people. Lunch is never boring.

I walked in one day, this book on my mind as I had been writing up a storm the night before, wanting to make sure the things I was writing were to some extent biblically sound. So, to the two pastors in the room I posed this question:

'If the Garden of Eden is a representation of heaven – '

'Is it?' The senior pastor asked.

'Isn't it?' I replied.

'Is the Garden of Eden a real thing?'

'Good question, but maybe a discussion for another time. My question is, if Eden was real and is a representation of heaven, being in oneness with God, then will loneliness exist in heaven because it existed in Eden?'

The children's pastor chimed in with, 'No, loneliness is a sin.'

A little surprised by her comment, I responded, 'Is it?'

'Well yeah, loneliness comes from a place where you have taken your eyes off God. You aren't relying on him,' she responded.

'The real question is – is there a difference between being alone and loneliness?' The senior pastor added.

'Hmmm. Good question. I'm going to have to think about it some more,' I replied, my head reeling with so many more questions but not knowing where to start. Their responses stayed with me for the rest of the day. I hadn't expected the conversation to unfold that way, but it did challenge my thinking about loneliness.

Before this discussion, I had never thought about loneliness being a sin. And I was not convinced.

I didn't think I was being sinful that night at the wedding reception. I was being real with what I was feeling. In fact, running to the bathroom was in a sense running to God. It was a place I could be alone with him and bring to him the deep pain I was feeling when I didn't want to take it to anyone else.

In my opinion, we need to not shy away from words like lonely. Loneliness may feel uncomfortable, but sinful? I think not. One of the fascinating things I find about loneliness is that it existed in the Garden of Eden. Loneliness was there before anything went wrong with the world. Right alongside love and grace and hope and kindness and compassion, loneliness existed with God and his creation from the start.

'The LORD God said, "It is not good for the man to be alone. I will make a helper suitable for him"' (Gen 2:18).

So, what is it about loneliness that makes us think it's a bad thing? Do we ever look at love or kindness or grace as a bad thing?

I believe there is a deeper purpose in loneliness.

If we didn't feel lonely, we wouldn't need each other, and we wouldn't need God. We wouldn't understand the depth of human connection. We wouldn't have an inbuilt mechanism that draws us back to God when we are feeling alone. Every time I have felt lonely, I feel as though I need to get out or get away, somehow physically change where I am or what I'm doing. In all its complexity, this is an emotion that I have found, more often than not, causes us to run to something, rather than away. And anything that is designed to propel us towards God can't be a bad thing.

The sinful part of loneliness sits within what we do with the moments we are feeling alone. You could take the feeling of loneliness to a bar or you could take it to God. You could give it a bottle of wine or you could give it a trusted friend. You could sit in solitude and let the bitter, negative thoughts consume your thinking, or you could take hold of your thoughts, as the Bible commands, and change the way you think. What we do with our loneliness matters.

The purpose of loneliness is not to taunt us about our lack; rather, it is designed to highlight our need. Our need for each other. Our need for God. Our need to not walk through life alone.

Loneliness is what reminds us that we need human connection. It's the driving force behind our desire to be seen and known. We may hate how loneliness feels, but it's the very feeling that can drive us towards greater connection, greater understanding and greater growth.

Is it uncomfortable? Yes!

Do we like feeling lonely? No!

Does loneliness propel us into connection? Yes!

Could that be the purpose of loneliness? I believe so. I think God, who knows well this deep desire for connection, knew what he was doing when he created us with the same need (connection) and the ability to yearn for it (loneliness). But he left it up to us to decide on what we would do about our loneliness when it rears its ugly head.

A lonely Jesus

This is where Jesus provides the perfect example.

Jesus experienced deep loneliness, not just when God abandoned him on the cross but for most of his life. Think about it. No one on earth could truly understand what it was like to be Jesus. He was misunderstood by so many people, even his disciples, all the time. Yet this did not deter him from reaching out and pressing in, especially to those who experienced loneliness in greater levels, like the sick, the oppressed, the forgotten. Jesus' depth of understanding of loneliness drove him to reach out to those who also knew what it was like to be cast out.

So, if Jesus knew loneliness in ways we can never understand, is it possible God has a purpose for this feeling within our story of singleness?

I believe the answer is a resounding 'Yes'.

In all instances where we can identify a sense of loneliness in Jesus' story, we see him reaching out, either to God or to his friends, to fill that gap. We see this in the moments when Jesus would remove himself from a crowd of people around him or send his disciples ahead of him while he took time out with God. It's quite possible that Jesus, fully God and fully human, felt loneliness in crowds of thousands because no one there would have completely understood what it was like to be fully God and fully man.

Probably the most perfect example of Jesus responding to those feelings of loneliness is in the Garden of Gethsemane. He gathers his friends to accompany him to pray while he seeks God in response to the burden that only he can bear. He then reaches out again to his friends who have fallen asleep, asking them to wake up and continue to support him in his hour of need.

This was something I didn't do that night at my friend's wedding. How different might my evening have been if I had simply allowed my loneliness to lead me to a friend, rather than only fleeing to the bathroom and hiding what I was going through. I went to God first in the bathroom stall, pouring my pain out, but I didn't do the second part of what Jesus models for us in Gethsemane. I didn't ask for support from my friends. What I have come to understand of those moments where we are deep in loneliness is that we need to seek out God, but we also need to seek out community – trusted friends and family who can pray for us while we wrestle through our trial.

Loneliness should propel us to take action, but this is only possible if we're willing to acknowledge that it's there, have the courage to push through the shame we might feel about it and stop hiding it.

Don't run from your loneliness. Don't be crippled by loneliness. Invite the light in and see how God will show up in ways you never thought possible.

THREE

Rejected

I recently read this quote from an interview between Lisa Messenger, editor-in-chief of Collective and author of *Risk and Resilience*, and Australian fashion designer Camilla Franks. In it, Camilla says:

'I've stared rejection in the face countless times, but I refused to accept it. It has made me stronger and fight harder. I've walked my own path and one that is mine and mine alone.'[1]

Could it be that simple?

At the time of reading that quote, I was holed up in a cafe in Melbourne, licking my wounds as yet another attempt at entering into a relationship had come to nothing.

I had met Lucas through a bizarre connection involving a podcast and LinkedIn (who needs Tinder, right?). The challenge was that he happened to live on the other side of the world, despite being Australian. I normally wouldn't have pursued anything, given the distance, but what started out as a couple of LinkedIn messages grew to texts and phone calls, and we discovered we actually got on really well.

The more we talked, the more invested I became. I really cared about Lucas even though I had never met him. I tried to hold it as loosely as I could, but I also won't deny I had moments of dreaming that our first meeting was going to be amazing and we would quickly come to the realisation we were meant to be. There was even a point where Lucas told me he had very much fallen for me and was so invested in this. So, we arranged to meet because he was coming back to Melbourne for Christmas and planned a stop in Sydney on the way through. The more our connection grew, the more I felt certain this was definitely going somewhere.

But it wasn't long until I sensed things shifting a little.

It was the small things. Moments where it felt as though he was pulling back a little. Conversations that weren't as long. Texts that seemed a little short. Just small things that I told myself to not stress about – these were simply the difficulties of building a long-distance relationship. But there were moments where I thought he might be having second thoughts.

When we did meet for the first time, there weren't the sparks I had hoped for. We had dinner at my place because it was pouring with rain. The conversation flowed, but there was something missing. I chalked it up to nerves and jet lag, given he had only arrived that morning. He asked what we were going to do on the weekend, which further affirmed for me that maybe this was all just first date jitters.

I had higher hopes for our second date – a walk and a picnic. Conversation was not difficult for us, but I struggled throughout the whole day trying to figure out if he was interested in more than friendship. Given how easy it was to be in his company, I thought that perhaps we just needed more time together. We had built this whole connection long distance; maybe we had to be around each other in person for a bit before the connection really landed. I remained optimistic that what we had discovered over the last few months would translate to something more. On the drive home we talked about making plans for the following day, maybe doing something towards the coast this time. As I pulled up out the front of where he was staying, Lucas turned me and said,

'In the interest of being completely honest about where I'm at, I don't have any romantic feelings for you. I feel as though this is just a friend thing.'

Ouch.

That hurt. Partly because deep down I knew it to be true. We were great friends, but probably nothing more. But mostly because here I was, yet again, experiencing another failed attempt at a relationship. He didn't know it, but in that moment those words re-opened a wound I have wrestled with my entire life.

Rejection.

If there is one word I feel I am most familiar with, it is this one.

The sting of rejection is something we have all experienced in varying ways. As single people, we can often feel as though this defines our journey. After all, when you go on dates and work hard at relationships but constantly end up back in singleness, it's not too hard to arrive at the conclusion that maybe there is something wrong with you, fuelling the fear that, ultimately, you will never end up being chosen by someone.

I mean, there has to be something wrong with us, right? Something either within us or outside of us makes us unacceptable. Unwanted. Unchosen.

If only we could figure out what that thing was.

A constant narrative of rejection chips away at hope, strength and the belief that meeting someone and getting married is possible. And every time rejection slaps us in the face (because let's be honest, it feels just like a slap) we have to muster the strength to get back up again, maintain hope and find the courage to get back in the ring.

For me, I didn't want to keep fighting anymore. Rejection had won and I was done with fighting it.

To add salt to the wound, a couple of days after that conversation in the car, I boarded a plane for Melbourne, where *he* was. I'd purchased the ticket weeks in advance so that Lucas and I could spend more time together, making the most of his visit home. I arrived in Melbourne hurting, disillusioned, foolish for thinking it was going to be different this time, and feeling deeply rejected. It wasn't until that morning in the cafe in Melbourne, when I read Camilla Franks comment, that I realised I didn't need to let rejection own me. That maybe it could be as simple as viewing it as a choice.

Coping with rejection is tiring. And hard. And it's a choice.

Choosing again

The revelation I experienced that morning in the cafe, reading that quote, was not that I had allowed rejection to define me. That, I knew. Rather, my revelation was that *I had the power not to let it.*

My journey towards freedom from rejection is littered with mistakes and heartbreak, but I have finally come to the understanding that I have allowed rejection to be my narrative. I have allowed the damaging words spoken to me by some of the guys I've had a romantic connection with to be my source of truth. I have allowed men to speak words over me that screamed of their insecurity, but I absorbed it as if it were my own. I have rehearsed the rejection narrative over and over until it feels as comfortable as an old sweater and worn it to remind myself, and everyone else around me, that I am a rejected one. *No one will ever want me.*

Being rejected by someone, painful as it is, should be an opportunity for reflection. It gives us a chance to examine who we were in that relationship and how we behaved. It is a time to reflect on behaviour and belief systems. Yet most of the time, we use rejection as an opportunity only to critique ourselves, focusing on all the ways we might have been seen as the problem, the cause of our own rejection.

I was too fat… not pretty enough… too strong… too weak… too desperate… too picky… too opinionated… (Insert your own self-directed insult here.) I know, in some way, you have had the same or similar thoughts and conversations on repeat with yourself.

No matter which 'problem' becomes the focus, each one of these beliefs is birthed from the same narrative. It comes from a deep belief that I am simply not enough. This belief drives all of the rejection self-talk and ensuing self-defeating actions. You will see in the following chapters how this deep belief that I am not enough greatly influenced my choices in relationships and my attitude towards my singleness. So much of my experience in and out of relationships has been dictated by this false truth.

And when we cling to false truths like this, we get it so wrong. We attack our personality and chip away at who we are, because it must be us. We are what's wrong with our failed love-life. After all, we are the common denominator, right?

We tell ourselves that it was the other person who rejected us, they broke our heart, they walked away. But really, *we* reject *us*. I reject myself. I reject myself because I believe I am too fat. I reject myself because I believe I am not pretty enough. I reject myself because I believe I'm too strong. I reject myself because I believe I'm too opinionated…

I reject me because I reject so many parts of myself.

Within that truth lies deep power. Because once you become aware of how you live in constant rejection of yourself, you immediately have the power to re-write the story.

Anatomy of a jigsaw puzzle

Someone's rejection of you – 'I'm just not attracted to you' or 'I don't see a future with you' – is in actual fact entirely about them. In the same way that you have an idea of the person you want to spend your life with, so to do the people you date. If you don't align with what they are looking for, then yes, they will reject you. But not because of who you are. Not because you are defective or broken. It's because of their own preferences, their 'list' of what they are looking for. Rejection in the case of relationships is about pursuit of alignment.

Think of a jigsaw puzzle. You don't grab just any piece and jam it in. You try different pieces until you find the one that aligns with the overall picture in the section of the puzzle you are working on. It's not that any of the other pieces were defective, ugly or unworthy. They just didn't align with that part of the overall picture.

When I think about it like this, I feel immediately better – realising I just wasn't quite the right piece for someone's puzzle.

The ridiculous thing is, when it comes to my own puzzle, I have often given priority to the piece (my love interest) and tried to rearrange all the other pieces of myself to go around it. When a person has decided they're not into me, rather than thinking, 'Oh, they just don't fit right', I've acted as though I need to change the whole puzzle to make them fit. I've come to see how much I've rejected myself in the process. With this awareness, now I can hold onto my own bigger picture and consider whether rejection from one small piece really does say anything about my overall value or worth – or whether it's just a matter of poor alignment.

This is an incredibly freeing space to be in but also, in my experience, a difficult one to arrive at. We're not wired to immediately and objectively see rejection clearly. And I want to take a moment to acknowledge that every ending of a relationship is an opportunity for us to ask ourselves the tough questions and to accept our part in the relationship not working out.

I equally want to acknowledge that it's okay to feel what you feel at the end of a relationship. A break-up is not something to be rushed, but rather processed for however long it needs to be, and there is grace for whatever length of time that is.

But our goal should be to move through the rejection. To not set up home and live in a constant mindset of rejection, because the reality is, sweet one, that you (and me and everyone else) are in a constant state of change and growth. Take the lessons. Leave the experience. Move forward.

Appreciate the whole puzzle, who you are and the life you are creating with God. It may feel incomplete, but it is still beautiful.

FOUR

Forgotten
_____

I met Matt through my friend Chloe and initially didn't think much of him. Mainly because I was certain he was interested in Chloe. But at a party one night, he and I got to talking, and I realised we had *a lot* in common. My interest was sparked.

As the party wore on, someone had the bright idea of playing the MASH game (Mansion, Apartment, Shack, House). It's a spoof fortune-telling game, the one where you write MASH above a square on a piece of paper, followed by a list of cars down one side, names of guys down the other and random numbers across the bottom. Then you invite someone to play. Through a convoluted counting process, you whittle down all the options until you're left with a 'prediction' – the house, spouse, mode of transport and number of children your player's future holds. It's silly, but it's a bit of fun.

A few rounds had gone by before Matt and I joined the table. My friend Whitney, who was leading the charge on this game, glanced in my direction with a twinkle of mischief in her eye that I knew very well.

'How about we do you, Neridah?' Whitney exclaimed.

'Sure. I'll give it a go.' I smiled back at her.

She immediately began to set up the game, adding Matt's name to the list of guys, and off she went. Round and round, counting and crossing things off, until she arrived at (surprise, surprise) Matt as my husband. Apparently we would have twenty-one kids, live in a shack and drive a BMW.

'You guys should go on a date. It's a sign!' Whitney boldly declared, and I felt as though I was going to die of embarrassment.

Don't force me onto the guy, Whitney! I yelled at her with my eyes. Until Matt, looking straight at me, said, 'I'm keen if you are?'

Completely shocked, I almost forgot to answer. But managing to regain myself, I said casually, 'I am if you are.'

'Cool.' He said.

'It's settled then.' Whitney declared, before moving on to torment someone else.

I glanced in Matt's direction and caught his eye. We exchanged a smile before refocusing our attention on the game's next victim.

The game continued for a few more rounds, more people decided to call it a night, and soon enough Matt and I were the only ones remaining. I was so surprised at how easy it was to talk with him, and even more impressed with the things I was finding out about him. I wanted our conversation to keep going, but it was getting pretty late. I showed him to the door and thanked him for the chat. He said he'd had fun and he'd catch me around. And that was that. He left. He didn't once ask for my number and I was way too afraid to bring up the whole date conversation. So, I left it, thinking how nice it was talking to him, disappointed he did not ask for my number.

But he was going overseas anyway, I reasoned. Matt was Australian and home to visit his family for a few weeks before heading back to where he was living in Europe. So, for him to ask for my number made no sense. It's not like we could really start anything.

Fast forward a week or so, and my flatmate Chloe was holding a party at a local pub. I dragged my friend David along with me, secretly hoping that I would get to see Matt that night.

Walking into the pub, I scanned the room and could see that Matt wasn't there. A little disappointed but shrugging it off, I grabbed a drink from the bar and joined the group. Not long after, Matt walked in. My stomach did a little backflip of joy. I waited till he had grabbed a drink and was walking back to join the group to get his attention.

'Hi hubby.' I cheekily chirped.

He smiled and said, 'Hey! How are the kids?'

'A nightmare. They're driving me up the wall. I think it's your turn to take them for a while.'

Sitting down one seat over from me – David was sitting between us – Matt said, 'We'll have to figure out some sort of arrangement.' I smiled, and our conversation flowed from there. We chatted over the top of David for a while, at which point he got up and went outside to make a call. As soon as he stood up, Matt made a move into the now-vacant seat next to me.

And the craziest, weirdest thing happened.

In my spirit, I sensed God saying, 'This is your husband.'

My mind froze in that moment. Had that come from me, or was it from God? Unable to truly assess what I'd heard, I pushed it aside. Matt settled into the seat next to me, and I resolved to take it up with God later.

Matt and I continued chatting. The more we talked, the more amazed I was at how well-suited we were. We liked a lot of the same things and wanted similar things out of life. The conversation swung around to the night of the party, and by this stage I had built up some liquid courage.

'Yeah, sorry I didn't get your number that night.' He commented.

'I was a bit surprised that you didn't.' I replied.

'Well, I'm going back overseas in two weeks, so I didn't think there was any point.'

'A lot can happen in two weeks, Matt.' I smiled coyly. (I even surprised myself at how bold I was being – thanks to Mr Chardonnay).

Matt paused and looked at me, obviously a little surprised at the boldness of my response, but equally intrigued.

'Do you want me to ask for your number?' He said.

'Do you want my number?' I asked.

'Do you want me to have your number?' He replied.

'If you want my number, Matt, you're going to have to ask for it.' I retorted.

'Okay then, can I have your number Neridah?' He smiled.

'Of course you can. Thought you'd never ask.' I smiled back.

We swapped numbers, and shortly after, David came back and said it was time to go. As disappointed as I was to leave early, I was happy I'd spent a bit more time with Matt. I said goodbye, making sure he knew it was his turn to look after the kids, and left.

Walking back to the car, David commented on how I had spoken to that Matt guy for so long.

'Do you think you'll hear from him?'

Smiling to myself, I replied, 'Yeah, I kinda think I will.'

The following afternoon my phone buzzed. It was Matt, asking about the kids.

And from there, our relationship escalated very quickly. The next two weeks were spent in deep conversations, a date or two, and a late-night kiss the night before he left.

Is he or isn't he?

Despite what I thought God had said to me, I braced myself to not hear from Matt once he had returned overseas. But to my surprise, our conversations continued and began to evolve into phone calls, messages, Skype calls and emails. We built a deep connection, from pictures of what we'd been doing to the things we were learning about God. Every text message finished with kisses. Every phone call taking longer. Every goodbye becoming harder and harder.

Underneath all of this, I was exploring whether or not I had heard God correctly that night at the pub. The more I prayed and sought the Lord, the more I felt he was affirming what I'd heard and telling me that I just needed to be patient. I never breathed a word to Matt, partly out of fear and partly because I believed it needed to be God who prompted Matt, not me.

We were never officially together. Not once did Matt define the relationship, and I was too afraid of being rejected to bring it up. Yet I held tight to God, trusting that he had a plan. I pressed into all I had been taught about God – that he was the God of the impossible, that he could do immeasurably more than anything I asked or imagined, that he was a good Father who cared about the desires of my heart. I made a conscious decision to trust God and wait on his timing. There was a purpose to this crazy journey I was on, and I was determined to find out what it was. I had never waited so strongly or fiercely for anything in my life.

As the months wore on, my patience did too. Every time I was about to give up and walk away in frustration or impatience or fear of being rejected, God would give me a Bible passage or a quote that spoke directly to my situation. I had them all stuck to my wall:

I remain confident of this; I will see the goodness of the Lord in the land of the living (Ps 27:13).

God is not human, that he should lie, not a human being, that he should change his mind. Does he speak and then not act? Does he promise and not fulfil? (Num 23:19).

Trust in the Lord with all your heart, lean not on your own understanding. In all your ways acknowledge him, and he will make your path straight (Prov 3:5–6).

You name it and it probably featured on my wall. It was the only way I could remain on this journey, while our 'relationship' puttered around in limbo.

I finally plucked up the courage to ask Matt what he thought about our relationship. What were we building? Was this going anywhere? His response was underwhelming. He said he wasn't sure; all he knew was that he enjoyed talking to me and didn't want that to stop.

But he wasn't about to ask me to come to him, and I wasn't about to ask him to come back to Australia for me. I figured it was up to God to tell him to come home, not me. Matt had to want to come home because he felt called to do so, not because I had asked him to.

This weird dating/not dating relationship went on for about a year. I stayed in it because I believed God would help us figure this out – that he would ultimately bring us together if I could just stay focused on God and follow his leading. I was committed to trying to figure out what God wanted me to do. Each time I asked what he wanted, I felt the response was just to wait.

And then one day…

I can almost remember it word for word because of the huge, deeply painful effect it had on me and my life.

Matt sent me a text.

Hi Neri, just wanted to let you know that I've started dating a lovely girl from church so things will have to be different between us now. I know this may come as a surprise but isn't it good to know that God works for the good of those who love him.

My world crumbled in that moment.

I couldn't breathe. I couldn't fight the tears. My legs started to give way under the weight of my broken heart. But I was on a busy street, with people moving all around me. I somehow managed to keep it together long enough to make it back to my car, where the tears that were stinging the back of my eyes began to flow unceasingly as my heart broke all over again. I didn't know what to think or what to say; I was so confused and hurt.

I responded to Matt the only way I knew how – complete freeze out. The days after his message, he tried to contact me, sending me messages about how sorry he was, but none of it did anything to soothe the deep pain I felt or to clarify the billion questions rolling around in my head, not least of which was, *What the f**k, God?*

I was so confused and hurt, not just by Matt's actions, but by God's inaction. I thought I had waited well. I thought I had done all that God asked of me. And yet, I found myself in heartbreak, pain and deep, deep rejection. And that rejection felt as though it came from both Matt and God.

A few days later, I mustered up enough courage to respond to Matt. Even with the pain and rejection I was feeling, I wanted to make sure that I acted in a way that honoured God. I filmed a short video message for Matt, telling him that I was really disappointed, but that he was forgiven, and I didn't hate him. I wished him all the best and sent it.

Hi God, remember me?

I wrestled for a long time after this experience with Matt. It was incredibly difficult to process the pain of being so certain God had given me a word and having that not become a reality. I felt deeply forgotten by God and couldn't work out where it had all gone wrong.

This sense of being forgotten by God is a tension I still wrestle with today. What is the balance between having a desire (like for a spouse or children) and trusting God will – or wants – to deliver on it? Urging trust in God, the Bible asks, what father would give their son a stone when he asked for bread? But I have often felt as though God keeps giving me stones instead of bread. This was certainly how I was feeling after Matt. In my head I know I haven't been forgotten by God, but my journals speak of a heart that finds this a difficult truth to grab onto.

Have you ever felt as though God is answering everyone else's prayers, but not yours? If you're human and you're a Christian, I know your answer to that question will be yes. Watching your friends and family receive what you so deeply desire is really difficult at times. It can be made even worse when you think things are finally turning around only to discover nothing has changed at all.

Look at all the stars on my chart, God!

Getting left behind, feeling misunderstood and the string of disappointments can all pile up, forming the basis for a belief that God has forgotten about us. That our dreams, our desires don't matter to God.

It's so easy to slip into this way of thinking. Especially if we feel we have done our best to follow God, to honour him in every area of our lives. The Bible tells us that we are not forgotten by God; it tells us that he knows every hair on our head. A God who pays that much attention to me surely must hear and care about the desires of my heart, right?

I have noticed that when I am in this belief that God has forgotten me, I start to list out all the ways I have honoured God, in some weird way believing that if I show him my highlight reel, he'll pay attention to me. You know the list I'm talking about: helping out at youth camps and worship nights, serving on rosters, attending Sunday services, reading my Bible, praying, leading a Bible study group, faithfully tithing and so on.

Now, we all know our faith is not based on works alone but that our works are an expression of our faith. But if I have done my best to show my faith and live it out authentically, why won't God deliver on the one thing I truly desire? I'm doing my best here God – what more do you want? Surely I have enough gold stars on the chart now that it's time to get the thing I've been waiting for?

But I consistently miss the truth that our desires are not a reward for our good work. I'm a naturally driven person and I have come to realise that I function on a work and rewards system. Put in a productive day at work, and I've earned myself a wine with dinner. Smash it out at the gym, and I can reward myself with a cheeky chocolate bar. Follow God diligently and do my best to honour him, and I will receive the desires of my heart.

I hated science as a teenager, but I'm told that Newton's Third Law of Physics is that for every action there is an equal and opposite reaction. Meaning if I do X, then Y will always, without fail, happen. It's kind of how I viewed my faith for a long time: if I do all the things God tells me to do, I will be rewarded for it. Perhaps many of you will relate.

Except we worship a God who not only created this law of physics and can exist within it, but he also exists outside of it. In fact, he exists outside of every known law of the universe. It is the complex mystery of God. My point in getting all physics-y on you (yes, that's a made-up word!) is to highlight the infinite God we serve and the finite beings we are. What if our interpretation of X always producing Y is wrong? What if X (our faith expressed through our commitment to Christ) equals U or C or LMNOP?

While we can't know God completely, we can remove him from the box of understanding in which we try to place him. We can't take our list of 'good works' and wave it in front of God, trying to get his attention. This kind of approach will get us nowhere. It only leads us to the belief that God has forgotten us. We can't earn his blessing; we can't pry his hand open with how many Bible passages we know.

We can't force him to do what we desire with our long lists of how we're good people.

There was no defining moment I can think of that changed my understanding of how I'd been holding rewards-based expectations of God, looking to get the desires of my heart to know that he remembered me and cared about me. The experience with Matt definitely triggered my awareness of it, but at some point I surrendered my list of achievements. I gave up trying to grab God's attention, trying to tell him not to forget me, and instead rewrote the narrative in my mind to believe what the Bible tells me.

Truth is, our works do nothing to motivate God. If God should choose to open his hand of blessing, that's his decision. While that might seem a little demoralising, the opposite is actually true. It is incredibly motivating because it means his hand of blessing is not reliant on my ability to be a good person. I can be blessed regardless of a list. So, if I receive any good thing from God, it's purely because he loves me and for no other reason.

I am not forgotten. God knows who I am. He knows my name. He knows me. And he cares about my desires. Not because he uses them as a reward system but simply because he loves me. He withholds things from me, not because he has forgotten me, but because he knows and cares about me intimately. And is always, *always,* working for my good, even if I don't understand his ways.

FIVE

Confused

I breathed the sea air in deeply as the yacht bounced and bobbed along the crystal blue harbour. Sydney had shown up in all its glory, and I was loving being out on the water. My friend had won three hours on a chartered yacht at a charity auction, and we were all reaping the benefits. The booze was flowing, the food was delicious, and we were doing what I and my girls to do best – belting out the best of the 80s, 90s and now at the top of our lungs.

The boat anchored at a gorgeous inlet, and we wasted no time diving into the crystal clear, refreshing water. After our swim, my friends and I were sitting on the front of the boat sipping on champagne and chatting. The conversation naturally swung to men, women and relationships. Three of them were married, and one was a lesbian. None of them were Christians. As you can imagine, we've always had lively discussions about controversial topics.

'How's things with Justin?' One of them asked.

'Great. Really great actually. He's pretty amazing,' I replied, soaking in the sun.

'I bet he is. That man deserves a medal,' one of them commented.

'Why?' I asked, finding the comment a bit strange.

'Well, sweets, he isn't getting any from you, is he? So he deserves a medal having the stamina to stick around. Not that you're not worth it, sweets, just … it must be hard for him,' she replied.

'In more ways than one!' One of the others quipped.

I laughed. This topic always came up with these women, so I felt confident to handle it.

'Well, first of all, sex isn't everything,' I responded.

'Yes, but it is important. How do you know if you're compatible?'

'By getting to know each other!' I replied.

'But what if you get married and he is no good in bed?' Another quizzed.

'Well I guess we will have to deal with it, together,' I responded.

'I honestly don't know how you do it.'

At this I sat up. 'Look, it isn't easy. It's really hard to want some-thing so strongly and not act on it. It's not like we haven't come close either. But you know me, I just love Jesus too much.' I smiled back at them.

'Well sweets, Jesus better make you into one of those saints, because only a saint could do what you're doing!'

'Different denomination,' I replied, lying back down.

'What?' she said.

'Never mind, sweets.' I smiled. The conversation swung to the sex life of one of the other women on the boat, and I let it wash over me. There wasn't much I felt quali-fied to contribute, after all.

Let's talk about sex

Sex. One of the hottest topics in the world today – and probably the least talked about in the Christian culture.

If you have been around Christian circles long enough, you will know this is a topic of high interest but low engagement, because the generally accepted stance on sex before marriage is that it is immoral. We are given one message – *do not have sex before marriage* – and it doesn't leave much room for discussion. That's it. Just don't do it.

For this reason, I think it's necessary to discuss it.

I remember nights at youth group where dating and relationships was the topic of the night (notice it was never 'Let's Talk About Singleness') and inevitably, every time without fail, the question would come up, 'How far is too far?' I can't remember all the answers given by those poor youth leaders, who were just trying to serve their church and probably struggling with the very same ques-tion, but I do remember one that got trotted out regularly. It was something like, 'If you're asking that question, then you've gone too far.'

I can see what the leaders were trying to get at, but I can also see that this statement contains a lot of judgement and condemnation – and not a lot of help. The kid asking the question was probably genuine in their motives, but was shut down. In my experience, this has been the church's typical response to questions relating to sex.

On the other side of things, we have a society that constantly bombards us with over-sexualised images promising our lives will be better if we just give over to our deep desires, so long as we're consenting. Life looks great when sex is your focus. It can look beautiful. It can be fulfilling. Porn is easily accessible these days.

Condoms are sold in vending machines in the bathroom. Think you might be in a bit of trouble? No worries, there is a pill to take care of that. The one thing I will give credit to the world for doing well is *talking* about safe sex. They're not perfect at it, but at least it's openly discussed – unlike in the church, where the only form of contraception is to ignore your God-given sex drive.

There is a constant pull between what the world is telling us and what the church is telling us about sex. It's not a new battle, but is it one the church is winning?

We want to honour God, but we also can't deny that he has designed our bodies to desire sex. The world recognises that desire and tries everything to capture it, telling us that safe, consenting sex is perfectly fine. In response, the church yells 'just don't do it' a little louder, then buries its head in the sand. The topic of sex is relegated to the 'marrieds only' section of church life, as if somehow they are the only ones who want sex. Meanwhile, we're not equipping our single congregation members with meaningful theology and discussions that helps us navigate an increasingly permissive culture and our own drives and desires.

Digging a little deeper

But I, for one, want a fuller understanding of where sex fits into the world of the single person. As I came to write this chapter, I spent some time reading through various perspectives on sex before marriage and delved deeper into what the Bible has to say about it.

There are plenty of passages in the New Testament that speak of 'sexual immorality'. The most frequently quoted is 1 Corinthians 6:18–20, which tells us to 'flee from sexual immorality'.

This term is used as a kind of catch-all when it comes to any sexual act outside of marriage, but its meaning is imprecise. I needed to dive deeper. What I wanted to understand was how premarital sex makes it into the same category as adultery and bestiality, which are also consid-ered sexually immoral.

The Greek word used in the 1 Corinthians verse is *porneia*. If you're thinking this sounds vaguely familiar, it's because we get our modern day word 'pornography' from this root word. Throughout the New Testament, any time the term 'sexual immorality' is mentioned, the original Greek is *porneia*. However, the Greeks orig-inally used the word to refer to prostitution. So, why do our Bibles use the term 'sexual immorality' rather than simply 'prostitution'? Over the years, as the New Testament has been translated from the Greek into English, the word has been infused with broader mean-ing. Prostitution was considered sexually immoral, so translators simply took the essence of the word and started using the term 'sexual immorality'.

The million-dollar question is, what does this term actually mean? What does this catch-all phrase include? There's widespread agree-ment on few things, like adultery and bestiality. But some Bible commentators include premarital sex under the same umbrella, while others argue against this, given the original meaning of prosti-tution. I hunted around for a definitive meaning to the word 'immorality' because it seems to be the important part in that phrase, denoting what is right or wrong about sex. The term 'morality' refers to the principles discerning the distinction between right and wrong, good or bad behaviour. Unfortunately, this definition muddies the water a little more because our modern-day principles allow premarital sex so long as both parties taking part in the act of sex agree to it. To our modern-day society, this is not sexually immoral.

So the term 'sexual immorality' isn't really helpful in determining if premarital sex is actually immoral. The Bible doesn't explicitly say, 'thou shall not "Netflix and chill" before marriage'. It just keeps saying to flee from sexual immorality.

As I thought about this, I was adamant there must be something in the Bible that backs the argument that premarital sex is immoral, otherwise how have we arrived at the conclusion that sex before marriage is wrong? The only story I have found that lends itself to this argument is Deuteronomy 22:13–19, where it says:

> *If a man takes a wife and, after sleeping with her, dislikes her and slanders her and gives her a bad name, saying, 'I married this woman, but when I approached her, I did not find proof of her virginity', then the young woman's father and mother shall bring to the town elders at the gate proof that she was a virgin. Her father will say to the elders, 'I gave my daughter in marriage to this man, but he dislikes her. Now he has slandered her and said, "I did not find your daughter to be a virgin." But here is the proof of my daughter's virginity'. Then her parents shall display the cloth before the elders of the town, and the elders shall take the man and punish him. They shall fine him a hundred shekels of silver and give them to the young woman's father, because this man has given an Israelite virgin a bad name. She shall continue to be his wife; he must not divorce her as long as he lives.*

Now this passage at first seems to be talking about a husband slandering his wife and calling her unchaste just because he doesn't like her. But if we read the story for the moral principles found in it, we can see that there was a lot of weight placed on the virginal status of the woman. Virginity represented honour and purity and was very important because an unchaste woman ran the risk of ending up alone and possibly on the streets, begging for food. Women had very few rights and relied heavily on the protection of a husband. This is why the punishment for the man is to pay a fine and remain married to her.

Respect and honour were everything to a man. So, if his wife was not a virgin on their wedding night then she would bring shame on him and his household. No pressure, right?! (Interestingly, the man's virginity status doesn't even get a mention in the passage.)

But things are very different these days. Women no longer have to rely on the protection of a man in order to survive. Women's rights have come a long way since the Deuteronomy passage and a woman's virginal status doesn't carry the same weight as it did back then. Which brings me back to my question – where is the biblical reasoning to not have sex before marriage?

I seem to be hitting a dead end in trying to form a solid argument that we shouldn't have sex before marriage. It might be time to change tack. If I can't find a definitive verse to support the message to not have sex before marriage, maybe I need to look at why we should have sex in the context of marriage, because there's an abundance of examples showing that sex *within* marriage is definitely allowed.

We're told that God intends sex for marriage, and if that is God's best for us, then we need to understand what sex in that context looks like. Song of Songs provides the best insight into how God wants us to enjoy sex. The book shows us that love, respect, service, honour and forgiveness are what make sex great within a marriage.

Song of Songs also contains this striking verse: 'Daughters of Jerusalem, I charge you: Do not arouse or awaken love until it so desires' (Song 8:4).

This verse, again, is often rolled out as proof that the Bible does explicitly say to not have sex before marriage. At first glance, it's not hard to make that connection. But we need to take a closer look at the word 'love' used here. The Old Testament was written in Hebrew, and the Hebrew word used in this passage is *ahabah*, which translates to love, which is a very broad word. What type of love is it referring to here? Parental love? Platonic love? Sexual love?

Looking at the verse in its wider context, we can see that love at the very least refers to the love between a husband and wife. Is the young woman advising her friends to not be hasty in their pursuit of finding a spouse and to trust God to guide them? Or is she talking specifically about sex?

There's no definitive answer on this, but in my opinion it means both. When we look at sex throughout the whole Bible, we see a consistent narrative that it was designed for marriage. We see it from a cultural standpoint where a woman's virginity mattered. We see it in stories where the marriage bed is not honoured, and the result is destruction (David and Bathsheba). We see it in entire books, like Song of Songs, where the setting of the book is a marriage. Marriage is important to God because it's a covenant, and it's undeniable that covenant is deeply important to God. God set up marriage for us to experience covenant, and he placed sex within it so that we would be able to freely enjoy it.

So, God has placed sex within marriage, and Song of Songs shows us that sex is meant to be this wonderful, deeply vulnerable, serving and satisfying experience. It stands to reason, then, that sexual immorality is whatever is the opposite of what the Song of Songs shows us. Immoral sex is dishonouring, self-serving, degrading and hurtful.

The thing I find interesting about this is that sexual immorality is not only found outside the bonds of marriage. I have known Christian couples caught in the heartbreak and pain of pornography. Equally, I have known non-Christian couples who displayed deep love, respect and care for each other. (I seem to be developing a habit of proving a point and disproving it in the next sentence. Can you see how confusing this topic can be for Christian singles?)

But there is one key difference I have discovered that sets apart Christianity's approach to sex from the world's approach to sex, and it's this: we can't separate the physical act from the spiritual self.

Song of Songs highlights an important truth that is often missed or disregarded in discussions about sex, both within the church and outside of it. Sex connects us on a soul level to someone because it is deeply vulnerable, and it should therefore be treated with conscious respect, love and honour. It is literally the closest you will ever be with someone, and like you cannot separate the carrot from the carrot cake, you can't separate your soul from your physical being. Our spiritual selves are just as involved in the act of sex as our physical selves are. Questions like 'How far is too far?' are our attempts to remove the spiritual self from the physical act. When we do this, we remove God from it. I think this was what the young woman in Song of Songs was trying to communicate to her friends, that sex isn't just a physical act; it's also about our spiritual selves and an embodiment of love.

This is the difference between the world's self-gratifying, on-demand approach to sex and the Christian all-of-me, serving-the-other approach to sex found in Song of Songs. Our souls, our hearts, are the connection point to the Holy Spirit, the place we come to know and experience God. That is a sacred connection that should be honoured and kept for God and the person he has brought into our life to marry – someone who has proven themselves trustworthy.

So, do I believe that avoiding sex before marriage is wise counsel? Yes, I do. Even though the Bible doesn't say it explicitly, there is no denying that the act of sex is deeply vulnerable and deeply spiritual. When the Bible talks of 'two becoming one', I believe it speaks of all the ways two can become one: physically, emotionally and spiritually. In sex, we're intertwining our soul with another, and we can never take it back. This is exactly how God designed for it to be. And when he saw that it was good, he put boundaries around it so that we could really experience it in all its intended glory.

There you have it. To be honest, I set out to find that loophole. I really wanted to be able to find a definitive answer to this age-old question and be able to say, 'Yes, single person, sex is yours to enjoy before marriage because Paul didn't really mean that, he meant this!' I kept searching and came up unconvinced that the word *porneia* refers exclusively to prostitution or exclusively to premarital sex. It simply isn't clear enough, given the way we have infused meaning into the word over the years. Which is why the journey led me back to sex being more than just a physical act. Our spiritual selves are just as much a part of it and we need to honour that.

Where to from here?

It kinda feels like I've landed that last bit where we already were – don't have sex before marriage. I know, I'm a little disappointed too. It brings me back to my original question. Is that all we need to be taught? In some respects, the answer is yes. But I do think the church needs to do a better job at engaging in this topic in order to properly equip Christians singles to navigate the turbulent social waters of modern life.

Conversations like the one I had on the boat have been a regular occurrence over the years, especially with this particular group of friends. These women love me dearly, and I know that their questions are not filled with judgement or condemnation. I'm never made to feel stupid for believing what I believe. They may not understand it, but they love me regardless, which has led to rich conversation.

Truthfully, they have taught me so much about sex. Not simply the physical act of sex, but I hear in their conversations the importance of it being pleasurable for both parties and how they have advocated for that in their respective relationships. I hear acceptance over someone's sexual preference and equal encouragement for that person to talk about sex. I hear laughter over moments where things didn't go as planned. I hear growth, and I hear grace. I hear women trying to figure it out in a healthy way. I see in them that the act of sex outside of marriage or the Christian context is not about the individual and their satisfaction, but that it can be really loving and self-sacrificing, regardless of religious affiliation. It has helped me to understand that sex isn't this bad thing that suddenly becomes amazing when there is a ring on my left hand. It is a deeply satisfying experience when practiced and explored within a healthy, supportive and loving relationship.

God's version of what that looks like, a supportive, healthy, loving relationship, is marriage. Unfortunately, the church waits until marriage to discuss sex, and even then it doesn't do it very well.

Some Christian friends have shared with me how their wedding night did not live up to their expectations because for years they had been told not to do something, and no one ever talked about it – and then all of sudden they were 'allowed to' but they were completely unprepared. Their brain needed time to catch up. Just like the church needs to catch up in order to adequately address the reality of sex within our society. Sex needs to transition from a taboo topic to one that is openly discussed. Sex is a deeply personal thing, and the discussions need to happen in a way where single and married alike do not feel weird or ashamed to ask questions or seek advice.

We can no longer ignore sex or hide from it, for risk of completely losing touch with the world God has placed us in. My hope and prayer is that the church will begin to bring something as wonderful as sex into the light and respectfully discuss it with both married and single people. Singles need to know that it's worth waiting for and why they should be waiting for it, and not just have 1 Corinthians 6 thrown at them when they are seeking counsel. Single people need to be supported and encouraged as they manage the now and not yet of sex – and equally, to be loved through their choices around it. We need to be offering, and offered, grace and acceptance for whatever someone chooses to do with their sex life. Because God does.

Let's talk about sex. Let's talk about why it matters that we experience it in the covenant of marriage. Let's talk about what's good about it and what's bad. Let's talk about how sex is more than just the physical act. Because us singles need more than just a blanket answer. We need to know that refusing to arouse love until God intends it will be worth the wait.

SIX

Jealous
———————

Ugh. Okay, I'm going to go there.

This is one story I'm not proud of. It's about falling for a guy who didn't want anything serious with me and the subsequent jealousy that infused my brain, rendering me insane. At least, that's how I would plea in a court of law if ever it went before a judge: insanity. Because that's what jealousy leads us to – a display of completely out-of-character behaviour as we seek to grab hold of that which we want.

This is not my finest moment, but here it is.

I had known Sam for a long time. Or rather, I had known Sam's reputation for a long time. In the same year as me at youth group, Sam had managed to break the heart of at least three of my friends already. He was very good at making a girl feel as though she were the only girl in the world. But other than periodically hating on him from afar for hurting my friends, I never had much to do with Sam until I started at uni.

Sam and I went to the same university, and he was a year ahead in his degree. In the lead-up to me starting, we chatted a bit about the university, and he was really kind and very helpful in answering my millions of questions about it. During the first semester of uni, I spent quite a bit of time with Sam and his friends. They subsequently became my friends, and I got to know Sam more. The more I got to know Sam, the more I saw girl after girl fall for him, only to have their heart broken. I don't think Sam was intentionally seeking girls out to break their hearts – I think he just liked the chase.

As I observed this over the course of a couple of months, as well as knowing Sam's past with my friends, I started to feel as though I should say something to him – lovingly, as a sister in Christ, of course. Perhaps I ought to give gentle rebuke and hopefully be the one, as a sister in Christ, to guide him to treating his sisters in Christ better. Maybe it was for such a time as this that Sam and I had become friends. (I was *so very* spiritual!)

So, I arranged to hang out one day after classes were done. I drove us to his favourite beach, we had some dinner and as we were sitting on a park bench, I told Sam that I felt God had given me a word for him. Sam needed to be aware of how he was treating God's daughters. I remember talking for a few hours about how he really needed to think through how he flirts with girls, how he might be leading them on with the way he treats them. To his credit, Sam took it well. And I, of course, was a willing friend and offered to help in whatever way possible so that he would not break any more hearts.

At the time, I was convinced I was doing the right thing. Now, however, I can see my motives may have been less than pure.

Following our talk, things were fine with Sam, but I wasn't exactly sure how much good our chat had done to change his behaviour. The more I saw Sam continuing to lead girls on, the more frustrated I got. I couldn't quite put my finger on why, but it annoyed me. I hated seeing my friends being led on, and I hated it even more now that I'd told Sam he needed to think about his behaviour. I figured I was reacting out of loyalty and care for my friends.

Then one night, it all became clear. In a moment of pure weakness, Sam and I kissed. Like all good love stories, it happened at a Christian music festival after everyone had gone to sleep and we stayed up whispering in the corner of the tent. I can't remember what we were talking about, but I succumbed to his charm, nonetheless. By the end of the evening, I had myself believing that this meant Sam wanted to be with me.

What I thought might have been the start of a relationship with Sam soon turned into the realisation that Sam had just wanted some fun, which made me feel so foolish for thinking he liked me or that this changed our relationship in anyway. Adding salt to that gaping wound was the realisation that I had feelings for Sam – and I'd had them for some time.

All of sudden, the reality hit that this was why I had always been so annoyed with him flirting with girls. I wanted to *be* one of the girls!

Although I had cloaked it all in Christian piety and even convinced myself of my spiritual motivation, each step I had taken up to that point had been because I was jealous. I wanted to be wanted, like Sam had made those girls feel wanted. Even though I knew he was a heartbreaker, I still thought that maybe I was different. I wasn't. Which made me mad and jealous when I saw Sam flirting with other girls. This jealousy brought out the worst in me. I was judgemental of both Sam and the girls he pursued. I gossiped about him and those girls. I was deeply jealous of any girl who became close with Sam. I made silly decisions, like putting myself in a position with Sam where I ended up with my heart broken.

Needless to say, after a year of liking him and being deeply jealous, I finally woke up and walked away from the hope that Sam and I were going to be anything. He didn't want anything more with me, and God graciously brought me to the point of being able to see that clearly, enabling me to walk away. We did remain friends, however, and it was an honour to attend his wedding to one of my other dear friends, someone who was truly a great match for him. Yet I will never forget the jealousy I felt during that time and the way it completely changed my personality.

When the highlights are on repeat

No one wants to admit they are jealous, but can we just be real for a moment and be honest, at the very least to ourselves, that we all suffer from it? Jealousy is one of those feelings that kind of brings out the cray-cray in all of us. And because of that, we don't like to own up to the fact that we are feeling it.

It really is a powerful emotion, one that can completely skew and blur our vision of reality, leading to surprising behaviour. For single people, jealousy can very easily creep in. It doesn't take much. An engagement announcement. A baby shower invite. A couple's holiday post. The person you have a crush on dating someone else. Any of these things can have us plummeting into the depths of jealousy because someone else has what we want, and all we can see is our lack of it.

We spend so much time looking at other people's highlight reels, then we compare it to our reality and only see what we don't have. The art of comparison is never helpful when it comes to humans. Yes, compare prices of cars or your insurance or different hotels for your holiday destination. But don't compare your life to someone else's. It's not a fair comparison.

As a single person, I think this might be the emotion I feel most ashamed of. Jealousy does not bring out the best in us; instead, it produces bitterness. It reveals a weaker side to our character, our lack of satisfaction with our lives and our frustration at our inability to control things. Jealousy causes us to behave in a way that isn't God-glorifying. At its extreme, it produces the vindictive behaviour that we see on popular reality TV shows like the Bachelor; at its most basic, it produces gossip and slander. Jealousy only produces more pain, more hurt and more suffering for us. It leads us to dark places like despair – and despair is where hopelessness resides.

And yet, the antidote to jealousy is so simple. Shut your eyes. Okay, not literally (we're likely to do some damage that way), but figuratively. We need to take our eyes off other people's lives. This might mean limiting our interactions with social media. Or stopping engaging in conversations about other people. Or even withdrawing from unhelpful social situations. In my case, with Sam, I put distance in place in order to truly move past my jealousy. I began to focus my attention on other friends, investing time and effort into people that were going to point me more to towards God and help me release what I thought I wanted.

However it plays out, the point is that jealousy does not need to bring out the crazy in us if we simply stop looking around and start looking inward – if we start dealing with what's going on inside rather than what's going on in someone else's highlight reel.

Change you, change your life

I once heard this very interesting saying: 'If you want things in your life to change, you have to change things in your life.' Kind of obvious, yet profound. This puts the power straight back in our hands. By looking inward, instead of at how everyone else has an Instagram-perfect life, we empower ourselves to create change. Then we can funnel that energy into something productive rather than wasting it on the coveting treadmill.

Comparison is often what creates the negative lens through which we view our singleness. We start to see everything as working against us. No matter how hard we fight, we can't seem to win. And when things don't work out, we default to jealousy. We can end up in a cycle of bitterness, frustration and anger at our situation, constantly blaming everything and everyone around us.

How do we stop this cycle?

For me, I had to take off the lenses through which I was viewing this whole area of my life so I could finally see clearly.

It took looking at these very real things I was feeling – loneliness, rejection, feeling forgotten, fearing that no one understands, jealousy, despair, deep sadness – to see that maybe they didn't have to keep me spinning on the bitter merry-go-round I was on.

Maybe, just maybe, they could be a catalyst for growth.

The Context of Single Me

SEVEN

Not Everything Given to You Is Useful for You

I could see her bite her bottom lip ever so slightly, like the words she wanted to say were on the tip of her tongue, but she was not letting them out for fear of my response.

'Go on, just say it.' I said.

'Well, people find you intimidating. You're very strong, and maybe that's why you can't find a guy. You're too strong.'

That single sentence, spoken to me by my well-intentioned-but-blunt friend pushed me over into a pit of despair. So, I *am* the problem. Who I am is not good enough; or rather, who I am is *too much*. I need to change. No one will ever want me if I am this strong person. Strength is not an attractive quality to guys, and I intimidate them. I need to stop being strong.

How the heck do I do that? I thought, despair filling my spirit.

Has anyone else received advice or comments like this? (I see that hand! And that hand! And that hand!)

As if dealing with the array of emotions we feel as singles is not enough, we also have to navigate the turbulent waters of advice from friends, family and society. Although usually delivered with good intentions, the advice our nearest and dearest throw at us can be deeply hurtful and unhelpful. It leaves us scrambling to hide the wound that's just been inflicted while trying to glean what truth there might be in what's been said.

There is a difference between healthy advice and unhelpful opinion. The Bible instructs us to seek out and soak up wise counsel (Prov 12:15; 15:31–33). Sound advice is objective in nature and delivered in love. Opinion is thrown around and too often delivered from a place of ego, making the one giving the advice feel good that they could finally say what they have been thinking for a long time. It's basically judgement masked as help.

Our challenge is to discern between advice and opinion.

My friend's comment about being 'too strong' is opinion. For her, at the time, strength seemed an unattractive quality to men. She was not wrong in her comment – I am a strong woman – but her error lay in the opinion that my strength is a bad thing, particularly if I want a relationship. I received her opinion as a message that I needed to change.

Which was true. I *did* need to change, but not by removing my strength. Rather I needed to embrace it, understand it, learn to harness it – because God had given it to me. He had crafted me to be this way. It just needed a bit of refining.

I've heard it all by now

Married friends and family can often miss the mark with their comments, suggestions and questions. How many times have you experienced any of the following? I imagine it's too many times to count!

Unhelpful questions:

- Why are you single? (If I knew why, I wouldn't be single now, would I?)
- Are you putting yourself out there enough? (If I put myself out there any more, you'll be asking me if I've backslidden!)
- Do you think that maybe you're too independent? (So I should sit at home and wait for someone to call?)
- Do you think that maybe you're too strong? (So I shouldn't have an opinion and use the mind that the good Lord gave me?)
- Have you prayed about it? (Only every moment of every day of my life. How about you?)
- What's wrong with people? You're amazing. (Thanks, but yet another question I can't answer and can't do anything about.)

Unhelpful comments or advice:

- Maybe you just need to let guys know you need them (So, be weak and needy then?)
- Don't be weak or needy (…wait, what?)
- When you stop looking, he will just appear (*shuts eyes* Is he here yet?)
- Don't be too picky, you're not getting any younger (Thanks, I'd forgotten about the biological clock that ticks and gongs incessantly every time a friend announces they are expecting.)
- God is just preparing you, you're still a work in progress (I didn't realise we needed to make it to a certain level or state of humanity before we were suitable for marriage.)

- Don't be so obvious about your feelings (But I'm meant to at least show my interest, right?)
- Wait three days before you text (Right, so be unavailable…)
- Respond straight away so they know you're keen (Hang on… be more available?)
- The guy should always pursue (But what if he is completely clueless?)
- Maybe the reason you're single is because of some sin in your past (…)
- Make a list and pray every day over it (I did that in the tenth grade, and nothing has changed.)
- Don't date them unless you're sure you're going to marry them (But isn't the point of dating to figure out if they are someone you could wake up next to everyday with terrible morning breath?)
- Change churches if you're not meeting anyone (Because finding a husband is the only reason I attend my church?)
- Focus on your 'marriage' to Jesus, he is your true husband (But Jesus doesn't cuddle.)
- Focus on being a Proverbs 31 woman (What even *is* flax?)

The list could go on and on. I include it so we can laugh a little at the absurdity of it all. But I also hope it can help us to catch ourselves or others out if we hear these kinds of statements bandied around. A deep desire of mine is not just to encourage single Christians to stay the course on this crazy journey, but to help our married friends and family become more aware of how they interact with the single people in their lives.

On that score, I've decided to turn the tables and provide some helpful advice to well-meaning friends and family so that they can feel empowered to be a support to us.

Let me help you help me

Dear married friends and family,

You're fun and awesome and provide examples for us. As you navigate the minefield of marriage, we watch on, observing and learning. For some of us, you could be the closest reference to a healthy marriage we have. So please know that what I'm about to say doesn't come from a place of bitterness or anger or jealousy but rather from the many, many conversations I've had with Christian singles who are feeling a little frustrated.

It is true, we were all single at some point in our lives. Your journey towards your marriage might have been difficult or easy, but either way it was your journey and it was real.

But your journey is your journey. The three steps you followed to find your partner, or the way you fasted and prayed, or how you did nothing at all – worked for you, which is great. But just because it worked for you doesn't mean it is guaranteed to work for your single friends. Sometimes the advice you give, based on your own experience, may not be relevant for where your single Christian friend is at.

Yes, we know that you used to be single, too. But anytime your life makes a monumental shift like marriage or having kids, things change, and you are no longer the person you were moments earlier. You might try to convince yourself (and those around you) that you haven't changed, that you still understand the old life, but the reality is you have transitioned from one stage of life to the next. There's no turning back.

In fact, to your single friends you begin to become unrelatable the moment you say, 'I do' (I would even argue as far back as 'so I met someone…'). Sure, you were single until you met your partner three years ago, but you haven't been single for three years. Memories fade, seasons shift, and let's be honest, the moment you knew your relationship was going somewhere you were probably relieved to know that you were no longer 'one of us'.

I don't say that with any malice or bitterness, just an acceptance that unless you are still single, you don't really know what it's like to be anymore. So, if you want to share your wisdom with me, your advice needs to shift from 'I get it, I know exactly how you feel…' to 'That sucks. That is really hard. I admire your courage to keep going. Don't lose heart.'

It's worth checking in with yourself why you're offering that bit of advice in the first place. I'm a big believer in the idea that if someone wants your advice, they will ask for it. Yes, they may be sharing their story or their heart with you, but that doesn't mean they want you to start sharing your thoughts on what they should do. Most of us just want to be listened to.

I often talk to people, not because I want a problem fixed but because I need to get something off my chest. I'm pretty sure I am not alone in being a verbal processor. When we verbal processors speak with you, we're really preaching to ourselves. We're talking ourselves off the ledge. We're seeing the situation more clearly just by talking about it.

There's an old saying: 'you have two ears and one mouth, use them proportionately'. It is wisdom I try my best to adhere to. The desire to provide a single friend a list of suggestions, steps and how-to's usually stems from wanting them to know that they are not alone. But it can actually have the opposite effect.

Instead of asking your friend why they are still single or providing advice on what you think they should do, a better approach might be to encourage them.

How are you encouraging or honouring the single person's commitment to Christ?

How are you honouring or encouraging them to tread their own path in this relationship journey?

How are you honouring and admiring their courage to stay committed to the journey?

I used to think that asking married couples 'When are you going to have kids?' was a good, well-thought-out, relevant question, until close friends of mine struggled to fall pregnant. It took a while, but I started to realise how hurtful a question like that could be to a couple. Because the issue wasn't about having kids; it was the wound that would get pressed on every time 'when' was used. They didn't have the answer. They didn't know when. They were hopeful, but – as many couples have experienced with infertility – there's no guarantee. A question like 'When?' can be really hurtful.

In the same way, asking someone why they are single can be hurtful. The reasons to be single are varied, from choosing to be single for a period of time to focus on God, to a deeply painful heartbreak, to lack of opportunity, to loss of a spouse. Asking 'why' a person is single is not be the best place to start. Nor is asking what someone is doing about it. I have never once asked my married friends who say they want kids, 'Well what are you doing about it?' partly because I don't want to know, but mainly because it's none of my business. Should they choose to share their struggle, then I can listen and encourage. Otherwise, I keep my mouth shut.

Maybe you believe you have great intuition or perhaps spiritual insight, so that's where you're coming from with your advice. Maybe. But I believe in a God who is infinitely creative. And while two love stories can be similar, they are rarely ever exactly the same. As a friend, you don't know when or how (or even if) God will answer your single friend's prayer. You can hope for them, and you can believe for them, but you have no guarantee. As I experienced, even a 'word' from God is no guarantee, because God chooses not to control us, rather allowing us to make our own decisions and co-create our own lives.

So, I've just shared what not to do when it comes to your single friends. But we know you love your single friends and want to be there for them. Here are some things to consider if you want to truly offer support.

Be aware of their particular vulnerabilities (loneliness, rejection, despair) and ask them how you can love them well. You may think you know how they want to be loved, but I can vouch for many when I say coming over to your place for a coffee and giving us only a fraction of your undivided attention because the kids are going nuts does not make us feel loved. Ask your single friend what it looks for them to feel loved. Don't assume or anticipate, just ask. Commit to loving them that way, then actively do it. Your single friend will love you back for it.

Check in and get consent before trying to set your single friends up. Your single friend may be going through a stage in life where being in a relationship won't work for them. Or perhaps they have decided to be single for a very specific reason. Either way, don't go about setting them up on blind dates or chiding them about choosing to be single unless you have spoken to them about it. Ask if being in a relationship is something they want right now. I guarantee you, the ones who want to be in a relationship will be open about it and probably be more receptive to the idea of being set up. For those singles who want to be married, your network of friends and co-workers could be the pool of talent they have been looking for. And if you do promise to set them up, turn around and deliver on it! Building up false hope is hurtful, not just to them but to your friendship. 'But let your "Yes" be "Yes", and your "No", "No". For whatever is more than these is from the evil one' (Matt 5:37 NKJV).

Finally, show them that you benefit from their company, that they are more than a great backup babysitter or someone you only touch base with after church on Sunday but never invite over for lunch. Show them that you love their friendship, that you feel challenged by them and their friendship means something to you. There needs to be an equality in the friendship.

A bit of thought and sensitivity can go a long way in cultivating meaningful relationships and communities with us, your single friends. Rather than trying to fix us or our situation, sit with us. Commiserate with us, be joyful with us, believe with us, and above all encourage us to walk out our unique journey when it comes to finding a spouse.

Love,

All your single friends and family.

P.S. When it comes to putting money in for group presents, count yourself as two people, not one. It means your single friends won't have to pay more just because you're in a relationship.

EIGHT

Do Me a Favour; Don't Do Me a Favour

'DAD' flashed up on the screen of my phone. That's a bit odd, I thought. Dad doesn't normally call me in the middle of the day.

I quickly answered and was a little relieved when his voice sounded bright. He was just ringing to tell me that a man he knows named Craig was interested in knowing more about one of the organisations I work for, and would it be okay if he passed on my details? Of course, I replied, happy to help in any way.

Dad also mentioned that Craig's church was hosting an event that coming Saturday and had suggested I come along, because that way Craig and I could chat about his work. I wasn't free on Saturday night but told Dad he could pass my email onto Craig and I'd see what I could do.

The following day, Craig sent me an email, enquiring about my work. I found the tone of the email a little strange. I responded that my boss was the best person to speak about what our organisation could do for him and that I would connect them both, which I did.

The day after, I received another email from Craig. He was sorry if he'd come across a little strong in his first email, but he wasn't sure if his question really warranted my boss's time. Would I be interested in coming to this event on Saturday night so he and I could discuss things further? *Hmm,* I thought. The event was an hour from where I lived, and I couldn't see the need to drive all that way to talk about work. This started to seem a little strange.

I called my Dad that night and relayed the conversation to him. He agreed that this was really strange. At which point, my mother chimed in with an 'Oh.'

'What does "Oh" mean, Mum?' My suspicion started to rise.

'Well … Craig is the kind of guy who likes to connect people. I just wonder if there is an ulterior motive to him asking you to this event.'

'Do you think he wants to set me up?' I responded.

'Well, maybe.' She replied, a little sheepishly.

'What? He doesn't even know me. We've never met! Why on earth would he want to set me up?!' I fumed.

At this point my Dad fired up, annoyed that he had put his daughter in this position and annoyed that his friend had not been entirely honest with his intentions.

'I'll call Craig right now and tell him to back off!' He said.

'It's all right, Dad,' I said. 'I'll handle it. I'll call Craig tomorrow and suss out exactly what is going on.' We said out goodbyes and hung up. I sat there in disbelief. This didn't make sense. Why would someone who doesn't know me, has never even met me, try to set me up?

The absurdity of the experience was about to go up a notch or twelve.

The following day I called Craig. I began the conversation by explaining to him why my boss was really the best person to speak to, especially because he had specific experience in the industry Craig worked in. But Craig kept pushing for me to come to this event so we could talk.

Starting to tire of the merry-go-round, I asked Craig, 'What exactly do you feel you need my help on?'

'Well, I guess it would be how to deal with a Board of Directors. Which is why I think it would be great if you came on Saturday night, there will be lots of people there. People in your situation. [This remark got my attention immediately]. It would be great if you came and could talk to some of these people.'

That was it. 'People in your situation' was the tipping point. I thought to myself, *I'm going to make you say it.*

'Could you give me context around these people you want me to speak to? Is it a youth group or something?'

'Well, ah, no. Well, really… it's just one person.'

Finally, ladies and gentlemen, the truth.

'Who is this person?'

'Well he's a really great guy… ' and Craig proceeded to rattle off all the credentials of the guy he wanted me to meet, concluding with, 'He's a very good friend of mine, but I haven't mentioned a word of this to him. I think it would be great if you came along on Saturday night. I don't know if you drive out this way, but I'd be happy to come and pick you up and drop you home.'

That last part almost tipped me right over. Pick me up? I'm thirty-five! I'm a very independent, capable woman, and I can drive myself – *if* I choose to go somewhere.

I took a breath and paused. If I knew his friend's name, then I could at least look him up online and see what I could find.

'Would you feel comfortable telling me your friend's name?'

'Oh, ah, yes – yes I would. It's Nathan of the Smith family.'

Being someone who tries to be open to God working in truly mysterious ways, I responded, 'Okay, Craig. I'm actually busy on Saturday night, but why don't you send me the details of the event, and if I can somehow swing it, I might make an appearance.'

'Oh great. Yes. I'll send a message to you with the details,' Craig fumbled on. 'Maybe we could talk again tonight as well? I'd like to chat with you further.'

For what purpose I had no idea, and I was running late for a meeting, so I needed to get out of this awkward situation and end the call. 'Well I'm not sure what time I will finish tonight, but why don't I text you later.' Craig agreed to that, and we said our goodbyes.

On my way to the meeting, my head was reeling. I couldn't believe that this was happening. Some mate of my Dad's, who has never even met me, gets in touch out of the blue under the pretence of wanting to connect over my work when in actual fact he wants to set me up.

The whole thing felt really weird and really uncomfortable. But in the spirit of giving it a go, I pulled out my phone and cracked open the best stalking tool I owned – Facebook. After a bit of searching, I found Nathan's profile. It didn't tell me much.

Bummer.

As I sat there replaying the conversation in my head, I realised that the whole thing just didn't feel right. I was not okay with putting myself so far out of my comfort zone to go to an event where I knew no one, only to be stuck talking to someone who sounded like they didn't have much in common with me.

So, I made the decision to not go on Saturday night, even though I could have moved some things around to make it happen. I believe that what is meant for me will not pass me by, so if Nathan and I are meant to meet, it could happen in a less forced and strange way.

I opted not to call Craig that night, telling him instead that I would speak to him the following day. I did update my parents on the latest conversation I had with Craig, which fired my Dad up again. The encouraging part was that my parents backed me up. They agreed it was a very strange, weird thing to do and that I shouldn't have to drive all that way just in case I hit it off with someone.

The following day I set out to end this weird scenario and called Craig one last time. I explained that I couldn't come on Saturday night. I also told him I believed that if Nathan and I were to meet, it would happen organically, in a way where we both felt comfortable.

'Oh yes!' Craig responded, 'Well, maybe I could have you over for dinner one night and invite Nathan as well.'

face palm

'That feels a little forced as well, Craig.'

'Hmm, I guess you are right. Well what if you and I developed a friendship. What if we got to know each other a better, and then that way it might happen organically?'

I was clearly not getting my point across.

'To be honest, Craig, I wouldn't feel comfortable investing in a friendship that had an ulterior motive or expectation. I would feel huge amounts of pressure to make something work for fear of disappointing you, so I don't really feel comfortable with it.' *That, and the fact that you're a sixty-five-year-old man with whom I have nothing in common!* I thought.

Craig continued to push for a friendship for a few more minutes, but eventually got the point that I was not willing to play ball. I thanked him for thinking of me and wished him all the best. As I hung up, relief flooded my body. Another ordeal was over.

If only I were kidding

This story often earns the response of 'Are you kidding? I can't believe you had to go through that. I'm so sorry'. I laugh it off every time, but the reality is there is no shortage of stories like this circulating among the Christian singles I know.

Well-meaning friends and family (or in this case, friends of family) set out to do you a solid and connect you with someone they think might be a good match. There are plenty of stories where these scenarios work out. And then there are plenty of examples, like my mate Craig, where the well-intentioned person misses the mark entirely and actually makes the reality of singleness worse.

How many times have you been set up by a well-intentioned friend who should never have tried their hand at the match-making business? Or went about it in entirely the wrong way?

I'm not against friends or family keeping an eye out for us singles. I'm against it when they haven't really thought it through, are doing it from a place of pity or trying to make something happen because they have dreams of standing up at your wedding and proudly saying, 'If it wasn't for me then none of us would be here today…'

This experience with Craig made me realise that our married friends and family quite often have good and noble intentions but fail in the execution. I've had friends set me up at weddings without my prior knowledge or permission. I've had friends text me out of the blue wanting to connect me with someone, not stopping to ask if I even want to be set up.

What I realised through this experience was that, while I needed to have grace and kindness towards Craig and his well-meaning intentions, I also needed to trust my instincts and not apologise for them.

I'm normally someone who is all for giving things a go, because sometimes people can surprise you. Through this season of singleness, however, I have come to have a clearer understanding of what I truly want out of marriage. I believe that God is directing my steps and that what is meant for me will not pass me by. He directs my steps not just through his word or the people he places around me, but through my intuition. Through the Holy Spirit within me. Opportunities will present themselves, but if it doesn't feel like it's a good fit or something feels off, then I need to back myself and have the courage to say 'No'.

And I trust that by saying 'No' now, I'm ultimately saying 'Yes' to someone else down the track – someone more aligned with who I am.

NINE

The Debate of a Soul Mate

My first year out of high school, I served on my church's youth camp. I had been on it many times before, but this year I was part of the 'Servant Squad'. This put me into deeper connection with some of the youth leaders that year.

I remember one conversation I had with one leader, a young woman I had never really spoken with before. The topic of boys came up, and I said something along the lines of wanting to meet 'the one'. This leader, who was married, turned to me and said that she didn't believe in soul mates or 'the one'.

This caught my attention. I had always thought that if God knew the number of hairs on my head, then he must be just as intentional about who I would marry. He knows me best, so he knows who's best for me. *Ergo*, soul mates are a thing. To hear that this leader disagreed had me intrigued, so I asked her why she thought that way. She told me that neither she nor her husband believed soul mates were a thing. Instead, they agreed that they could be with any number of compatible individuals, but they chose to be with each other. This, she explained, made it even better than a soul mate, because you were really choosing that person. It wasn't predetermined, it wasn't fate – it was a choice.

This confused my young mind because it raised questions around predestination, free will and how involved God truly is with our lives. I remember discarding her opinion, believing too deeply in love and soul mates. I was very much a hopeless romantic!

I love the idea of a soul mate – I really truly do. I grew up in the Disney era where Prince Charming fell in love with you in the morning, defended your honour and saved you in the afternoon and by the evening you'd be married and riding off in a carriage to live happily ever after. Or if Disney isn't your thing, the Christian version would be meeting at the morning session on a youth camp and placed into the same Bible study group as your crush, where he wows you with how much he knows the Bible. By the afternoon he would have asked you to go for a walk where you talked about God and your missionary dreams. At the night rally he would sit next to you, and by the end of the evening you both would have received a word from God that this person was 'the one'.

I am, however, a recent convert to the line of thought that we don't have a soul mate. Part of the reason is because I've realised that the 'soul mate' I would have picked for myself at twenty-five is definitely not the same 'soul mate' I would pick for myself at thirty-five. Who I am has changed and evolved. Could I have found a great guy, an equal match to do life with, at twenty-five? Absolutely. Could I find a great guy, an equal match to do life with, at thirty-five? Absolutely. Would it be the same guy if I met him at these separate times? Quite possibly not.

The whole soul mate idea has us pinning our hopes of lifelong marital happiness to a single person, who we are somehow able to recognise as 'the one'. But what if I'm having an off day when I meet him? What if it was before my morning coffee, and I'm so grumpy he thinks I'm a horrible person? What if I take the car instead of the train and therefore never sit next to him, we never strike up a conversation and he never asks me on a date? There is so much pressure to get it right and make sure we are switched on enough to identify who this person is.

The concept also implies that this person is going to be the person who connects with you in ways no one else ever has or will. They truly get you. They understand you. They love you for all that you are. Your relationship will be perfect because you are a perfect match. You will find absolute marital bliss and joy because you have found the one person you're meant to be with, your happily-ever-after ending. No wonder we love the idea of a soul mate when this is the picture painted for us.

Reality, however, is different. At any stage of our life, we could find someone who seems like 'the one'. But I wonder if we just call them a soul mate because, at that point in time, that person is the ideal partner for us? I think those people who have been able to find love twice (or more) in their life, like those who find love again after a spouse has passed away, would say so.

The belief that there's only one person I could ever be truly happy with is a little scary. And to think that I have only one shot at finding that person feels like a lot of pressure.

God, the ultimate puppeteer?

Remember that belief I had about God knowing the hairs on my head and therefore planning my perfect match? I've realised that this belief places all of the responsibility on God to deliver this hand-picked man, relinquishing me of any role, as though I don't have the ability or the smarts to choose in partnership with God. I see now that this belief has a payoff; it means that if anything ever goes wrong in this area, then it must be God's 'fault' and not my doing. While the belief sounds good – our God is a very intentional God – it removes my role as a co-creator and active player in my own life.

That God is intentional about our salvation and the development of our character, I believe is truth. But what if – and I'm honestly still pondering whether or not this is true – God is intentional with some very specific areas of our lives, while in others he simply allows us to join him in co-creating our lives? He allows us to accept responsibility of our choices. He works with us to bring about his best while allowing us to exercise free will.

If we're made in his image, then surely we're made with enough creativity to craft and mould our lives? Surely we have agency for co-creating with Christ?

Remember Lucas, the guy I met on LinkedIn? We looked great on paper. My feeling is that, given the right context and time, we could have worked out and had a great relationship. There's even the real possibility we could work out now. Both of us had a desire for a lifelong partner, and both of us presented that desire to God. God took that request and worked his will out for us to meet, but ultimately Lucas decided that this wasn't what he wanted. He exercised his free will, and we went our separate ways.

This experience challenged me deeply. What if everything I'd believed about how God 'works' was wrong? I have spent my life constantly pestering God for words and signs on how to behave in the pursuit of a relationship. My preference has been for God to take control and puppeteer me into marriage, sacrificing entirely my personal actions and choices, because I simply have not trusted myself.

The Debate of a Soul Mate

Can I be trusted to be of sound mind and make my own decision in alignment with God's will for my lives, especially when it comes to finding a spouse? Do I have enough strength to say no to myself in order to wait for a person who is not perfect but aligns pretty well with what I'm looking for, at the right time? Because of the particular church culture I grew up in, which has left me with a deep fear of getting things wrong in the dating department, these have been new questions for me.

More recently, it dawned on me that my constant need for guidance – asking God to tell me what to do when it comes to relationships – might actually be the wrong approach. I have willingly exercised my free will in other areas of life, making choices for myself, feeling confident enough to trust that the decision aligned with God without constantly seeking signs of his approval. But in the area of relationships, I have been driven by a fear of getting it wrong.

But I can also see that sitting underneath the fear of getting things wrong is a fear of being hurt. If God is calling the shots, I can't get hurt, right? But I've come to recognise (and experience) that God doesn't guarantee a life of no pain; he guarantees that we won't go through pain alone. Learning to trust myself, my free will, means learning to be okay with pain because, as I have shared, there have been plenty of times when I have gotten it wrong. God didn't keep me from the pain; he came through it with me. The pain has helped shape me over the years, so much so that I'm no longer approaching relationships with a pain-avoidance mindset. I know now that pain is a part of the journey and regardless of what happens, I'm not alone.

The reality is, God has given me free will, and I have a choice in whether or not I will exercise that gift. I have a good head on my shoulders, so I should use it. God trusts the intelligence he gave me. I can trust the heart and mind God gave me and move towards potentially painful situations, knowing he is with me always, both to comfort and to guide.

More importantly, God trusts his Holy Spirit within me. Thankfully we are not left to our own devices to navigate life; we have been given the gift of the Holy Spirit who acts as our trusty guide. There are times where the Holy Spirit will prompt and direct me. There are times where I will receive flashing neon signs. There are times when a still, small voice will whisper. And there are times where it will feel like there's radio silence. Not because God doesn't care, but because he has given us a mind that he wants us to use. So, I'm starting to trust that if I make a poor decision, he will let me know through the power of the Holy Spirit. And if I still go ahead and make a poor choice, he will be there to pick up the pieces as I allow him to heal my heart and refine my character.

Is it God's best for me?

I went for a really long walk in Melbourne recently with a friend. We weaved our way through parkland, industrial areas, roads, train tracks and a really dodgy park where we feared for our lives, finally arriving at Port Melbourne. As we walked, we did what we always do and discussed many of the big mysteries of life. Both being single at the time, the conversation inevitably swung towards dating and marriage. I asked my friend what his views were on marrying a non-Christian, anticipating the typical Christian response, 'Do not be yoked together with unbelievers'. Instead, he made this great comment:

'I don't think it's as straight forward as "should I or shouldn't I?". There are so many examples where both scenarios have worked out. I just think of it like this: could I date a non- Christian? Yes. Is it

God's best for me? Probably not. Either way, it would be my choice and I would have to live with it.'

I found this such a helpful set of questions. Rather than asking God, 'Is it okay if I date this person?', what if instead we asked, 'Could I date this person? Yes. Is it God's best for me?'

Could I do this? And is it God's best for me?

Turning the question back on us engages the mind God has given us. These two questions first cause us to consider our will, and then they cause us to consider the will of God. Holding both answers up against each other highlights whether or not we are aligned with God in this decision.

I think maybe we can trust ourselves a little more. I'm not saying we should throw caution to the wind, start carving up the dance floor, drinking ourselves silly and dating whoever we want. What I am saying is that maybe we need to take the pressure off and come back to basics. Come back to simply getting to know someone without the question, 'Is this my soul mate?' hanging over our heads and trust that in all things, God is guiding us and equipping us to make good decisions.

Maybe we could be each other's soul mates

There's an episode in *Sex and the City* where Carrie turns thirty-five. Single at the time, she organises a beautiful dinner at a fancy restaurant with her friends. Except, the evening doesn't go as planned. No one shows up to her dinner, leaving Carrie to experience a string of embarrassing moments with the wait staff. Completely dejected and understandably depressed, she eventually heads home. But Charlotte shows up at her apartment and drags her to the cafe where Carrie, Charlotte, Miranda and Samantha always have brunch.

Over a cup of coffee, Carrie laments about how she is thirty-five and alone.

'It felt really sad not to have a man in my life who cares about me… no special guy to wish me happy birthday… no soul mate… And I don't even know if I believe in soul mates.'

The girls sit with her, understanding what she is feeling without saying a word. Then Charlotte says something that has become one of the defining moments of the series – and something I feel we, as Christians, need to embrace. Charlotte leans forward over her coffee and says,

'Don't laugh at me, but maybe we could be each other's soul mates. And then we could just let men be these great, nice guys to have fun with.'

If soul mates are a thing, why do we have to find that in the opposite sex? Is it possible for God to have created soul mates to be just that – a soul we connect with who is a deep, life-long companion and friend? Does it have to be gender specific? Could friends or family members be our soul mates instead of romantic partners?

As Samantha says, 'Now that sounds like a plan.'

If we remove the mentality that our soul mate must be our spouse and start to see anyone really as a possibility, this alleviates the pressure. If we also remove the expectation that God should puppeteer us into the perfect relationship and instead start to trust our own hearts a little more, knowing God is guiding us, all of sudden peace starts to usher its way in. We can relax. Chill. Take the crazy down a notch. We can start to be at peace – and in peace is found the best version of ourselves.

TEN

The Idol of Marriage

The count was at five and I was increasingly losing interest in the sermon. So far, I had counted five out of five sermon illustrations about marriage and children in a sermon that was about the Holy Spirit. I left church that day feeling deflated. While I could understand the overall concept of the sermon, the delivery left me disconnected. I felt alienated by the illustrations, so the message didn't land in any deep way. Most of the congregation that day would have disagreed with me – but then again, the majority of them are married with kids.

I don't envy pastors. I imagine it's hard to be the shepherd of a flock, trying to be relatable to everyone. But I also don't let them off the hook easily. The church has often promoted a picture of the good life as one where you marry young, stay married your whole life and produce children. What I have witnessed is anything but that. I have seen great Christian marriages. I have seen what seemed to be great Christian marriages fall apart. I have seen non-Christian marriages become shining beacons of light, displaying what deep, true connection is all about. And I believe in a God whose only Son, when he was on earth, didn't even get married.

And yet, the church tells us that the best life is one where you marry another Christian and have kids.

This vision can be very alienating for those of us whose life has not unfolded this way. What's more, the church sometimes speaks about singleness in ways that are degrading and deflating, as though we single people are in limbo and cannot truly 'step into calling' until we are married.

Christian theologian, pastor and writer Dani Treweek, who has conducted her doctrinal research on the topic of singleness within the church context, says this:

> *By teaching that marriage is natural and normative for Christian adults, we have increasingly come to regard the single life as the exact opposite – unnatural and abnormal. As a result, the Christian who has remained single beyond what we deem to be and 'appropriate' amount of time is often considered to be leading an aberrant Christian lifestyle.*[1]

I can resonate with that sentiment, because I've bought into it. I read back over journal entries in which I've cried out to God for a marriage that would be a force to be reckoned with for the glory of God. There may be some beauty in that desire, yet it contains the subtext that I could not be a force to be reckoned with for the kingdom on my own – as though this could only be achieved through marriage. I've viewed my singleness as something to be tolerated until my real life could be begin.

I now see differently. I believe I am just as powerful on my own and can achieve great things within that. But this dialogue, this belief that is outwardly spoken by pastors and inwardly, subconsciously perpetuated by the church, is causing damage.

The day I found out I was a terrorist

I came across this quote in my research for this book, and it just about made me cry.

> 'The most devastating attack on marriage is coming today from singleness. Singleness is an assault on marriage… I just see singleness as a disaster.'[2]

According to the author of this quote, pastor and teacher John Macarthur – who in 1996, would you believe, shared a blog about the blessings of singleness – my marital status makes me a terrorist. (Apparently, I am launching a full-scale attack on marriage through my relationship status.)

The idea that people like me are out to bring to ruin the very thing most of us desire is completely twisted logic. I am not consciously remaining single in order to disassemble the institution of marriage. At this point in my journey, I am consciously remaining single *in order to prepare myself* to enter into a strong, deeply loving marriage. And I have a right to hold out for the best because I want to be the most useful to God. Rushing in or settling just to get out of singleness is not God's best and has the potential to derail me from what he wants to achieve through me.

I highly doubt that you would find one single person – yet-to-marry, divorced, widowed or otherwise – who is remaining alone in order to 'attack' marriage.

In our Christian subculture, we glorify marriage through the books that have titles such as *Not Yet Married*, *I Kissed Dating Goodbye* or *Quest for Love*.[3] All these books are about what to do while waiting for marriage, rather than about embracing singleness. I've read books that talk about marriage as a cleanser for our flaws, with the view that the single state is unable to substantially refine us in character. The assumption is that marriage will make you a better person. But really, any relationship can be an opportunity for refinement; it all comes down to the individual's willingness to change. Plenty of my friends have brought out in me the things that need to be worked on and purified. Just because someone is married doesn't mean they will change when a spouse highlights a flaw. A willingness to be refined is not restricted to marriage or developed in marriage – that responsibility lies with all of us, and all of our relationships hold opportunities for refinement.

We also place marriage on a pedestal through sermon illustrations and marriage announcements. How often do pastors use their marriage or family as examples in their sermon? These examples may well illustrate the point of the sermon, but if overused they can really alienate the single congregation members, who actually make up a significant proportion of the people sitting in the pews on a Sunday.

I find some of our typical church rituals around marriage a little alienating, like when a newly engaged couple is asked to stand so we can all applaud and congratulate them on their impending nuptials. It reinforces this idea that marriage is the goal for every Christian and doesn't acknowledge that singleness is a valid, honourable season of life.

I'm not suggesting we start running around congratulating people on being single. What I am saying is the way we publicly praise relationships and the approach we take to singleness needs to change. We need to stop looking at singleness as something to fix, or as a season that needs to be hurried through so your life can finally start.

A disease needing a cure?

The sad thing is that many of us single Christians have taken this narrative on and are busy trying to do away with the problem of our singleness in order to fit the church mould better.

Recently, I was out with some single Christian female friends. Over drinks, we were discussing how we should be more proactive in meeting new people. Someone threw out an idea that our church should hold a singles event with other surrounding churches.

The thought of this made me ill. I couldn't imagine anything worse. I stopped to think about why I felt this way, and I came to realise two things. I had lost faith in the church being a way to meet some-one, because if I hadn't met them in my twenties then the church couldn't help me. The second thing I realised was that I held a deep belief that even if such an event occurred, I would probably end up going home on my own anyway.

This led to another realisation. If we're going to change the narrative around singleness in the church, then the responsibility for change resides on both sides of the fence. Single people need to learn to fully embrace being single, own it, believe there is a plan for it and know that it is a good thing. And the church needs to change how it talks about, idolises and pushes marriage as though it is the ultimate life goal.

If we don't address this issue, then the church will continue seeing alienated single people looking elsewhere for a place to be accepted. As Dani Treweek notes, 'the number of never married and divorced individuals in our churches is half that within the community around us. This is one aspect of the contemporary Christian problem with singleness – our churches are disproportionately attracting and welcoming those in our wider community who are married but failing to do the same for those who are not.'[4]

Our dialogue about relationships needs to change within the church – and within ourselves. Rather than treating singleness as a disease to be cured or a season to be endured, are we willing to embrace it?

I've given church culture a pretty solid piece of my mind in these past few chapters, and my prayer is that there is a shift in the culture. But how quickly that happens or how embedded that shift can be depends on me. The work of truly learning to love singleness starts within.

# The Truth of Single Me

ELEVEN

Just When You Thought You Were Off the Hook, Single One

At the time of writing this book, I have been single for quite some time. Yes, I have dated and explored a few potential relationships, but for the most part, I have been solidly single.

This has not been a smooth ride. I have had highs – feeling as though singleness is great and fun and I'm enjoying it – and I've had lows – aching loneliness, past feelings of rejection surfacing, waterfalls of tears. Even recently, something triggered a fall into deep despair over my lack of a relationship, and it took *weeks* to crawl out of that pit. For a fair chunk of that time, I ignored God completely.

God has been here throughout. Beyond God, the one constant in my experience has been change. And in that, I have come to understand much more about the role I play in how good or bad this season of singleness can be.

Having read up to this point, you could be forgiven for thinking that I assume all my problems with my singleness rest entirely on external circumstances. Yes, as a single woman I've had my feelings dismissed, ignored and misunderstood. Yes, there has been some poor theology thrown around. Yes, the church needs to address the emphasis it places on marriage. And yes, my married friends and family need to think about how they support and love me on this journey.

But, dear friends, the buck stops with me. If I truly want to change how I feel about being single, how I walk this journey, then the reality is, *I* need to change.

I am the product of my environment. If you grew up in the kind of Christian subculture I did, you would have grown up with the mentality that the ultimate goal is to get married and have kids. We have had terms like 'soul mate' thrown at us. We've been encouraged to read books that gave us our ten steps to finding our partner and to do Bible studies that gave guidance, tips and long lists of do's and don'ts on how to find 'the One'. But for quite a few of us, 'the One' wasn't there to be found when we expected them to be. Were we doing something wrong?

I've spent so much time and energy looking at all the ways my life was 'wrong' that I couldn't see all the ways it has been right the whole time. I have come to realise that where I direct my focus determines my experience of anything. My experience of singleness has been so negative, in part, because of how *I,* as a single person, talk about being single.

The Bible tells us our words are powerful. 'The tongue has the power of life and death' (Prov 18:21). But we are so flippant in our use of them. Our choice of words matters much more than we realise, and it's time we start thinking about what we're saying, subtext and all. Dani Treweek puts it so well (again):

> *Why is this [the language we use around singleness] important? Well, if you think about it, you'll realise that in using this one-sided language we characterise the single life by what it is not (i.e. not*

marriage) and the single person by who they are not (i.e. not a husband or a wife). At even the most fundamental level of how we speak about singleness, we define the single life as a state of lacking, a state of deficiency.[1]

The way I have talked about being single is steeped in a sense of lack. As though I were half a person in search of my missing piece to complete me, rather than finding a piece that fits alongside me into the big picture of life.

Personally, I am not the biggest fan of the words 'single' or 'singleness', but I have thought long and hard about finding another option to refer to the state of someone not being in a relationship and there's no adequate word that I can find. As far as I can tell, no such term exists that truly communicates what being single is and means.

So maybe it's time we redefine the word 'single' itself.

How much is it worth?

My friend and I were at a bar recently, and as is generally the case with my single friends, we got onto the topic of relationships. I asked her if she was seeing anyone, and she replied no.

Then she said something that caught my attention, big time.

She said that what mattered most to her was character. The person she ended up with would have to have a great character, she said, because she was going to be sacrificing a lot for them. A slightly perplexed look rolled across my face as I pondered her words for a moment. I realised very quickly that she was right, and I loved how she had put it.

My friend has a great perspective on singleness. She truly values, treasures and protects her singleness. If she is going to let this valuable part of herself go and 'become one' with another person, then that person better be worth the sacrifice. I found this view so deeply refreshing, because it placed the value in what I believe is the right place – on the self. It is valuing your singleness enough to not wish it away as quickly as possible. It is being whole just as you are and not seeking wholeness from someone else.

This beautiful perspective is one that so many of us could do with adopting. If I'm going to sacrifice my single self to be in a relationship, then the person I'm doing that for better be worth it, because I will be giving up a lot to do so. If we can balance the scales a little more towards a positive outlook on singleness, to truly value what we have, I think we would all come to embrace and enjoy singleness a little more.

Being single does not need to mean pity-filled looks, lonely nights on the couch, or feeling locked out of some elite club. Single can mean so much more if we choose to add value to it.

We ascribe value to inanimate objects all the time. I have a Giving Key – an old brass key on a brass chain that has the word 'ROAR' engraved on it. Doesn't sound like much, right? For me, this key serves as a daily reminder that I have a voice and a message that needs to be heard. It reminds me of one of my life passages:

> *Speak up for those who cannot speak for themselves,*
>
> *for the rights of all who are destitute.*
>
> *Speak up and judge fairly;*
>
> *defend the rights of the poor and needy. (Prov 31:8–9)*

But it's just an old key. It holds no real value but for the value I ascribe it. So, when people ask me why I wear a key as a necklace (often followed by 'is it the key to your house?' or 'is that the key to your heart?') I don't try to pitch that it's a beautiful piece of jewellery. I tell them that it has great meaning to me and serves as a daily reminder of my calling and purpose.

What if we could change the value we ascribe to singleness?

What if instead of ascribing a low value to it, we ascribed great value to it?

What if instead of resenting this status that is part of who we are in this moment, we began speaking of it as a precious commodity? A time that is of great value. A season not to be rushed but to be relished. A time that should not be cast aside for just anyone or anything.

It's as simple as changing the way we talk. Instead of saying, 'There are no good single Christian guys/girls out there,' what if we tried, 'There are so many great Christian single guys/girls out there and I can't wait to meet them.' Shifts in the language we use change the way we see the situation.

I believe change is possible. I believe it's possible for the church to change its dialogue around marriage and singleness. I believe it is possible for our friends and family to change the way they view us, to change the way they engage with us.

But I also believe change starts with me.

I am the problem – and the solution

I cannot deny that I have been part of the problem I am speaking out against. I won't pretend as though I haven't tried to rush through this season. I won't deny there have been times where I have hated it with every fibre of my body, spoken so negatively about singleness, looked down upon it and lifted higher and higher the goal of marriage – to the point of idolatry.

I have kicked and screamed and yelled and well and truly thrown my toys out of the cot over being single in my thirties. I have been resentful of friends who found someone to be with. I have been rude towards married friends because I felt forgotten by them. I have lied about not being able to attend a baby shower because I couldn't stand the thought of being surrounded by babies and couples. I have been selfish and excluding, citing that my friends who are married or in a couple won't understand so there's no point inviting them. I have seen the worst of me surface because of jealousy. I have spoken incredibly unkind words to myself because I so deeply resented being single: 'No one will love me because I'm fat'; 'I'm such a loser'; 'No wonder no one wants me, I'm so hideous'. Such incredibly unkind things.

I will not deny I am the problem.

Which is why it's so empowering to know I am also the solution. Jesus says:

> *Why do you look at the speck of sawdust in your brother's eye and pay no attention to the plank in your own eye? How can you say to your brother, 'Let me take the speck out of your eye', when all the time there is a plank in your own eye? You hypocrite, first take the plank out of your own eye, and then you will see clearly to remove the speck from your brother's eye. (Matt 7:3–5)*

This passage is profound on two levels. The first is that we do need to deal with the plank in our own eye, especially because it's a plank and not a speck. We need to look at ourselves first before judging others. It's surprising to think we could ever see the speck in another's eye, given the blinding plank in our own.

So, what makes us able to see the speck in another's eye?

We see the speck and ignore the plank because the speck in the other persons eye is made of the same material as the plank in ours. In other words, if I am judging the jealousy in another's life, it's because I have huge amounts of jealousy in mine. I can see the jealousy in you because the jealousy exists within me. We often judge in others the very thing we dislike in ourselves because we dislike recognising ourselves in them. The only way we can see it in them is because it exists in us. Like can see like.

I know a girl who has completely walked away from God because she is so bitter about being single. Our mutual friend often updates me on how this girl is doing, and every time I have to resist the urge to cast judgement on her for giving up on God and letting bitterness take root. Why? Because I am so acutely aware of the bitter root that very easily springs up within me. I can recognise it in this girl because it is rife within me.

If I notice in others a trait I would like to change, I now know to look at why it's bothering me in the first place. What is causing the strong reaction in me? Why does it annoy or disgust or anger me?

And the answer, more often than not, is because they are reflecting something within me that needs to be changed.

A very wise close friend of mine often says to me, 'When the student is ready, the teacher will appear.' When he first said it to me, we were discussing an issue I had with someone, and I remember thinking, 'Yes, that's true, I guess I am the teacher in this situation.'

He must have known what I was thinking because he quickly followed it up with, 'And Neri, you never want to be the teacher.'

'Huh?' was my immediate response.

'You always want to be the student, because you always want to be learning and changing and never thinking you have all the answers. You don't know what you don't know.'

How profound. And annoying!

I like to think I have all the answers. I like to think I have a pretty good grip on life and how other people can change. But the older I get, the more I realise I know nothing. I understand nothing. And if anyone had room to grow and change, it is most definitely me.

Which is why it has been a relief to recognise my part in all of this. *I* have been the one who viewed my married friends as 'having it all', thereby elevating the position of marriage in my mind. *I* have been the one speaking rejection over myself, therefore expecting and justifying my rejection by others. *I* have been the one excluding married or couple friends from events, ultimately excluding myself from their lives.

Can you see how I was the problem? And equally, how I am the solution?

Can you see how you are the problem? And equally, how you are the solution?

True change comes through developing self-awareness. As I have become more aware of the negative dialogue within myself, I have been able to transition from seeing the glass as half empty to seeing it as gloriously half full. And it all began with a broken heart.

TWELVE

Welcoming Growth

I believe the greatest tool we can develop within ourselves is self-awareness. That may seem like a pretty big call, but I believe the degree to which we are self-aware is the degree to which we are able to grow and process any pain or trauma and move towards wholeness, healing and change. If we are unwilling to go within and honestly review what we're feeling, why we're feeling it and how that shapes our behaviour, then we remain in the mindset of being a victim of circumstance instead of the empowered child of God that we are.

What we believe determines our actions. Regardless of whether you are conscious or unconscious of your beliefs, every day you are operating out of your belief system. If you believe that the world is a horrible place, then you will only see the horrible things about the world. If you believe that you are not worthy of love, then you will only experience relationships that reinforce that belief and struggle to feel comfortable in relationships that don't.

When our beliefs are challenged, we are presented with an opportunity. And our beliefs about ourselves are never pressed on more than when a relationship falls through and we're thrust back into the world of singleness once more.

The one that finally broke me

I learnt a very big lesson a few years ago.

Life was good. I was feeling good. I was feeling strong and free, having made the decision a couple of weeks earlier to walk away from my entanglement with Matt, the guy I thought God had told me was going to be my husband. After doing that, I experienced such a release and had found a new zest for life. I felt ready for the next chapter.

And, as it turned out, there he was at church – back row, red jumper.

The service had ended, and I was mulling over what to do. It was a long weekend, and I was keen to maintain the holiday vibe I'd been feeling. My friend's voice broke into my thoughts. A group was heading out to dinner – did I want to join them?

We started to make our way out of church, letting more people know what we were doing as we passed them. Soon enough, there was a huge bunch of people coming to dinner. I heard someone asking who needed a lift. Spinning around to yell out that I had spaces in my car, I yelled straight into back-row, red-jumper guy's chest. I had no idea he was right behind me.

He looked at me and said, 'You're taking people?'

'Yep.' I said.

'Could I grab a lift?'

'Sure, no worries. I'm Neri by the way.'

'Justin.' He replied, and we shook hands.

Three of my girlfriends came up, asking for a lift. 'That'll make Justin the only guy – how you feel about that?' I asked teasingly.

'I feel pretty good about it.' He smiled.

All five of us climbed into my car, Justin scoring the front passenger seat because of his long legs. I was slightly annoyed at having to make small talk with a stranger, but given he was new to church, I reasoned that I should be nice. With my girlfriends chatting happily in the back, Justin and I got to talking about what we do for a living. The conversation flowed easily. The more we chatted, the more I thought this guy was actually pretty cool.

When we arrived at dinner, I hoped he would sit next to me so we could continue talking, but a mutual friend jumped in next to me instead. I felt a jolt of disappointment, but I squashed that quickly, resolving to let it go. After all, this wasn't going to go anywhere anyway. *It never does.* Immediately moving Justin to the friend zone, I set my mind to ignoring all hopes of anything more devel-oping between us and focused on something else. Anything else.

Dinner eventually wrapped up, and our friend Sarah suggested we all go back to her place to watch a movie. Justin asked if I could drive him back to church to pick up his car. I was a little disap-pointed that he wasn't going to be coming to watch the movie but agreed to take him.

As we drove back, I couldn't help but sense that maybe there was something there, some sort of attraction. I kept telling myself to not be silly. *Don't over-think it, he's probably just being nice.* I dropped him at his car. To my surprise, he offered to show me the way to Sarah's place.

'Oh, you're coming?'

'Of course, just wanted to pick up my car so I wouldn't have to come back to get it later.'
'Awesome,' I replied, 'I'll follow you then.'

Settling in to watch the movie, I couldn't help but notice that Justin made a concerted effort to sit next to me. Little bubbles of hope and excitement were rising inside of me, but I kept reminding myself to stop being silly. He couldn't possibly be keen on me. I sunk down deep into the couch, holding a cushion on my lap as the movie started to play.

Shortly into the film, Justin pulled the oldest trick in the book. Stretching a little, he casually put his arm around me. Well, kind of. It was resting on the back of the couch we were both sitting on, not touching me exactly. But it was still there!

Is he making a move? I couldn't figure it out. Again, I told myself to not be silly. *It's not a move, he is not interested in you, he's just resting his arm.* Focusing all my attention back to the film, I put the thought of him being interested out of my mind for a third time.

A moment or two later I felt the slightest touch on my hand, which was resting under the cushion I had on my lap. My heart skipped a beat. *I think he just touched my hand*, I screamed inside my head. There it was again. The lightest brush of my knuckles. That touch then became a little more intentional. It felt like a bolt of lightning coursed through my body. *Oh. Em. Gee. I think he* is *trying to hold my hand.*

Then his hand didn't just brush mine but started to work its way into mine.

Lift off, people! We have lift off!

I was no longer confused about whether or not he was keen. I was sure of it. And in that moment, the game changed.

We watched three movies into the wee hours of the morning and every time we sat down to watch another flick, Justin made sure he was sitting next to me, arm around my shoulders.

In between films we chatted, joked, threw pillows at each other and engaged with other people in the room. But as soon as the next film started, I was catapulted back into the electricity of our connection. Completely swept up in the sensation of Justin's hand holding mine, I barely paid any attention to the movies. I was being pursued, truthfully and openly. It was awesome. It felt amazing. And so, so different to anything I had experienced before.

When it became way too late for any of us to be up, we decided to call it a night. As we collected our things and said goodbyes, I lost track of Justin. I felt too awkward to stand around waiting for him after I'd said goodbye to the host, so I headed to my car. A moment later, I heard the front door close and turned around to see Justin awkwardly trying to pull his shoes on while racing after me.

Catching me just as I arrived at my car, he leant against it casually and, flashing that gorgeous smile of his, asked if I'd be interested in grabbing dinner some time. Trying to match his level of casualness, I said I'd really like that. He smiled again and pulled out his phone. 'Can I have your number then?'

'Of course.' I smiled back.

He gave me a hug goodbye, and we both got into our cars.

I waited for him to drive off before I broke out into a little happy dance. I had a guy who wanted to go on a date with me. And he was good looking. And we seemed to get on really well. And he wanted to go on a date with me. He *wanted* to go on a date with me!

And then...

Justin and I dated for almost ten months.

The first few months were wonderful. I fell hard and fast for this guy. I honestly thought he was amazing. He would buy me flowers regularly, take me out to dinner and do helpful things like transport furniture for me.

And then all the ways we were different started to surface, and those differences began to play on my insecurities. Things like he didn't like holding hands in church, but I did. He liked cycling but it wasn't really my thing, despite trying for his sake. He didn't need to spend a lot of time together, where I was all for hours of time in each other's presence. While these might seem small, insignificant things, they triggered my insecurities and prompted me to step it up in my girlfriend game. I started overcompensating. The more I felt us drifting apart and not progressing, the more I fought it. I figured it was me – I was the problem – so I did all I could to be the girl-friend I thought Justin wanted me to be. But this had the opposite effect. The more I tried, the further we drifted. Even though I could feel our connection waning away, I hung on for dear life.

Looking back, there were clear signs. But I just couldn't see them. Or rather, I didn't *want* to see the warning signs that Justin and I were not meant to be. I wasn't willing – because I honestly thought this was my only chance at love.

The day Justin broke up with me is still vivid in my mind.

I was on my way to get my computer fixed. I swung by Justin's place first; he'd agreed to lend me his external hard drive so I could transfer all my files to somewhere safe. Arriving at his front door to pick it up, Justin quickly ushered me out onto the street instead of welcoming me into the house as usual. *How strange,* I thought. He'd never done that before.

When we got onto the street, he turned to me and said that he didn't think there was a future for us, and it would be best to end things.

The world stopped turning for me in that moment. Everything came crashing down around me.

I threw question after question at him.

'How long have you felt this way?'

'But last week you said…'

'You don't want to fight for this?'

'You don't even want to discuss this? Talk about it?'

'What is the point?' He replied. 'I thought about continuing things until after your friend's wedding, but what would be the point?'

I couldn't hold the tears back anymore. They came hot and fast. 'I just don't understand. You made me think it was safe… safe to trust you.'

Silence. He had said all he wanted to, and I could tell there was no convincing him. Justin was done. That was that.

I was running late for my computer appointment by now. *How convenient for him,* I thought. I told him I had to go. He still lent me his external hard drive (what a saint!), and I got in my car and drove off. I made it around the corner before I had to pull over because I couldn't see through the tears. I dissolved.

I pulled myself together enough to make it to my appointment, hoping and praying it wouldn't take long. I just wanted to be at home, buried under my covers and forgetting the world. But I ended up sitting in the computer store for four hours, quietly crying to myself as I waited for my computer to finish backing up. All the while, the world kept turning.

I felt invisible. Alone. Rejected. And so very, very sad.

After our break-up, Justin and I never did resolve things in a satisfying way. Originally, Justin had offered to move on from church, given I'd been there first. Feeling that I should be the bigger person, I told him he should stay if he wanted. It was an act of graciousness I grew to regret. We continued to attend the same church for three years, and if I'm completely honest, it was three years of hell. I would feel anxious and sick every Sunday afternoon, always on alert and never really present when at church, keeping an eye out so I knew where he was in order to avoid him. It became clear early on that Justin was doing the same thing, taking the long way around just so he wouldn't have to pass me. Arriving late, leaving early, all to avoid each other. It was excruciating.

How did I lose my way?

The way that relationship ended, I have every right to feel like a victim. It was devastating to be dumped without consultation, without dialogue and without even being told why.

But I realised pretty quickly that the problems in our relationship weren't all down to Justin. They were also down to me. Painful as it is to admit this, I now believe that the biggest underlying issue in our relationship was my insecurity.

In the beginning I felt such validation from Justin. I felt pursued, desired, wanted – and not just wanted as a Plan B, the way it had felt with Matt, but wanted in all the best kinds of ways, all the public ways. I was his girlfriend. I wasn't alone. I wasn't just someone to fool around with. Someone thought I was worthy of being their girlfriend.

I was looking to Justin to counteract my deep belief that I wasn't enough.

Justin had made me feel beautiful because he pursued me. It was an incredible feeling, to feel desired, to feel worth the chase. But that was the problem. I was holding tightly to those feelings of beauty and worth, but I could only feel them through external validation. I never truly valued myself.

The source of validation began to feel threatened when I felt Justin start to pull away. The more the cracks began to show in our compatibility, the tighter I held on, twisting and contorting myself to fit what I thought was his idea of the girlfriend he wanted. I needed to avoid rejection at all costs. I wanted so badly to make it work, not because it was really that great, but because of my deeply held fear that this was my only shot.

In the process of trying to make this relationship work out at all costs, I abandoned my own internal sense of what felt healthy and right. On some level I didn't want to admit, I knew we weren't going to last, yet I decided that Justin must be worth contorting myself for. I had heard people say that love is a choice, and I vividly remember thinking to myself, *I consciously choose to love Justin.* I reasoned with myself that people say love is hard work, and so I was choosing to work at it. In hindsight, it was a dumb choice. Not because love itself is a dumb choice, but because Justin was not making the same choice to love me. My sense of self-awareness was so undeveloped, and all I knew was that I desperately didn't want to be single again. Justin was the best I had ever known and based on what I could see of my life, he was the best I was going get. I cringe thinking about what could have been if God hadn't pulled me out of that relationship. Thankfully he did, because if he didn't, I wouldn't have discovered the wonder of being me.

Discovering me

Following this break-up, I entered a very intentional season of singleness. I was so very broken, not just from Justin, but from Matt too. Without realising it, I was processing and navigating the pain from two break-ups and going through a baptism of fire which refined me in so many ways.

I have spent an uncomfortable, unwanted but completely necessary five or so years undoing the damage that was inflicted, partly by my own hand, in these relationships. It has been hard work getting to know my inner 'demons' – the insecurities I hold – and their origins. This process looks different for everyone (if we're willing to go on it) but for me it took the form of journaling, reading and honest conversations with friends. It started to become clear that I didn't value myself very much. I began to hear for the first time the way I spoke to myself and about myself, and I didn't like what I was hearing. I was mean, degrading and just plain horrible, constantly berating myself for all the ways I had made a fool of myself in relationships. This inner dialogue was what was fuelling my external need for validation. I needed people to tell me I was amazing, I was great, I was beautiful, I was worthy, because I could not believe it for myself.

Change is a choice. If I didn't want to repeat my past mistakes, then I needed to change. I took the first step and began to consciously shift the narrative loop playing in my head. When I became aware of a negative thought about myself, like looking in the mirror and saying to myself 'I'm so fat, who would ever want this', I acknowledged the thought and consciously replaced it with another. I wouldn't lie to myself; if I honestly couldn't bring myself to say 'I'm not fat', then I would opt for something that I did believe, like 'I really like my smile'.

I applied the same logic when it came to my relationship with God. I recognised that while I knew God cares about our desires, I believed he didn't care about my love life. In my low moments I would begin to take my anger, frustration and hurt out on God, telling him how much he didn't care about me. Which is a lie. Instead of letting the lie continue to take root, I swapped it out for what I did believe about God. Things like 'You're good, even if it doesn't feel like it right now'. Or, 'If you can part the seas for the Israelites, then you can help me find my way out of this funk'.

This technique seems so simple, but I think that is where its power lies. Like all things, change in mindset takes time and conscious effort. As I have learnt to love myself, I have grown in my belief that God loves me. There is a security that exists within that belief and even though there are days where the clouds roll in and I feel challenged again, I can weather those storms better because the bedrock of my belief has changed. Because I have taken the time to truly know myself, grow my self-awareness, value who I am and see myself as God has created me to be, I am in a much better place to actually love someone without expecting them to fill a need that was never their job to fill in the first place.

That is what I believe to be one of the sweetest gifts of singleness. As much as I was desperate to not go back here, if I hadn't, I wouldn't have been able to uproot those negative beliefs and replace them with truth. Singleness affords us the space for growing into who we really are.

I know, I know. You're thinking, *Ugh, that word – 'growth'*. I have a love/hate relationship with this word, too. Love the idea, hate the process. Because growth often means pain.

Take a plant. Until the seed cracks and breaks the shell it is encased in, it cannot begin to grow. Once it has cracked its shell, the little plant now needs to find its way through the soil, pushing, striving, reaching to the surface. Then when it reaches the surface, it has a whole new level of trials to battle – animals, the elements, humans – but it does not, at any point, despite the pain, stop growing.

Without something breaking, there cannot be growth within us. Without the pain, we cannot grow stronger, wiser, and more capable of dealing with the trials around us and the insecurities and negativity within. Like the seed, we're designed for growth.

I recently became a mother – of plants. It started with a Devil's Ivy, and an obsession quickly took over. One day I was watering my many plants and decided to move a tendril of my Devil's Ivy. As I did, the tendril broke off in my hand. I was devastated for about two seconds when I realised this break could actually be used to create more life and growth. I carefully cut up the branch, placed each little leaf in its own glass jar of water, sat the jars on the windowsill and waited. Every day I would check them, hoping to see the beginnings of a root forming, willing them to live, hoping I had done the right thing. It took time – a few weeks in fact – but slowly, little white roots began to sprout in the water. I watched as they pushed their way out, reaching for more water. I marvelled at how resilient they were, fighting to stay alive. Little did I know this was only the first battle.

Once the roots were long enough, I transferred all my little seedlings into individual pots, and my worry and concern over them heightened. I knew they were able to grow in water, but could they grow in soil? Only time would tell. At least in the water I could see their growth. But now that they were planted in soil, I had to trust the growth was happening. The whole process began again as I waited and watched to see if they would survive in this new environment. I'm happy to report that all of them are now thriving in their little soil pots. They have made wonderful gifts for friends, and the few I still have fill my house with so much greenery and life. Life that wouldn't have been realised if there had not been a break in the first place.

This is like the life I found after my breakup with Justin. That growth would not have been possible without the break in the first place, and I often marvel at what God saved me from and also what he planted me into because of it. I appreciate my singleness in ways I never thought possible. I embrace this time more lovingly than I ever have. It's not easy. Growth takes work, But what I've come to experience has been worth the pain. There is joy, wonder and awe to be found in singleness that I think few of us truly experience – unless we've been a little bit broken along the way.

THIRTEEN

Redefining Success

I was walking to work one morning, reflecting on my life. Thoughts swirled through my mind as I mulled over what I have achieved, the unanticipated things that have happened, the ways I feel I have lived a good life. Then this thought crossed my mind: *Obviously I have failed at relationships.*

And as soon as I had thought it, another thought (perhaps a prompting from the Holy Spirit) quickly followed.

What does success look like in relationships? And in singleness?

Opting to go down the rabbit hole of this question, I reasoned, *Well, success in singleness would be marrying someone.* Another thought countered that almost immediately: *Is that really true?*

This internal dialogue really struck me.

Why did I define 'success' in relationships as simply being in one? For that matter, why do I define 'success' in singleness as no longer being single? Is getting out of singleness really the definition of living a successful single life? And if it's not, what does success in singleness look like?

Part of the issue has been in the way I've defined success in relationship. Maybe you've never thought of relationships in terms of success or failure, but if you have had your heart broken, I'm sure those pesky feelings of failure have surfaced at some point and you've looked at others to see why and how they are 'succeeding'. I have often defined successful relationships by the outward fruit I see. The joy on lovers' faces. The way they finish each other's sentences. How they have been together for years. How I never see them fight. How they managed to find the love of their life at a young age. But these observations are fairly superficial. And we cannot define the success of a relationship based purely on such surface-level things.

A more reflective part of me knows that the success of a relationship is defined by the depth of connection. I've heard it said that intimacy is the most important thing in a relationship – 'into me see'. This deep knowing and being known is what we all desire and what God has shown us is the marker for a truly successful relationship.

But deep connection is not reserved only for marriage. We can have deep, meaningful connection in the relationships around us. Deep connection is about feeling fully supported and fully seen, that who you are is completely accepted. You need only be yourself. This kind of connection can take the form of a best friend, a close sibling, a dear grandparent. I have a friend who lives overseas, and our friendship is one of my most treasured relationships. I don't see her often or even talk to her that frequently, but it's one of my most beautiful friendships because with her I am fully seen and fully known. She will send me little notes and cards all designed to tell me I am loved and cherished. I can tell her anything and know it will be met with love and acceptance. She understands me, supports me and is always cheering me on. Our friendship is a deep connection that I will never let go.

The most important connections I have, however, are those with myself and with God. If I am not connected to myself and who I am created to be, then I don't know who I am, where my place is and what I bring to the world. What makes this connection possible and complete is knowing my Creator. In relationship with him I find truth, acceptance, forgiveness, joy and most importantly, love. I am fully known. Fully accepted. Fully seen. Apart from this, I miss out on the deeply grounding impact it has on my life.

It's very easy to think that the only relationship we will be completely accepted in is a romantic one. But this is such a limiting idea, because we miss the blessing of connection that can be found in the people around us and the Creator who made us.

The balancing act

My definition of being 'successfully single' has also shifted from a focus on how quickly I can get out of being single to how well I can walk through this season.

Success in singleness is like walking a tightrope with a balancing pole. On one end of the pole hangs the desire for a spouse, and the reality of our current situation hangs on the other. While it's tempting to lean towards one or the other, both ends of the balancing pole need equal attention and care if we're going to stay upright!

Perhaps like me, you've paid a lot of attention to the 'desire for a spouse' end of the pole and not so much to the 'reality of where I am right now' end. And perhaps like me, you are coming to see that accepting your reality will lead to a richer, more satisfying single season. But we are the only ones who can define what our own single season will look like.

If it's possible to 'fail' at being single, it would be through taking the lies, the loneliness, the hurt, the rejection and wrapping ourselves up in it, believing that it is our portion and we're never going to get out. Maybe we never say those things out loud, but deep down in our hearts many of us have a belief system made up of them. It's like a loop track, playing on repeat the lies that I will never be enough, there are no good guys out there, I'm going to be alone forever, and so on. We define ourselves by what we lack rather than by what we have, and consider getting paired up and married our ticket out of failure.

But getting married is not success – that's just transitioning to another season. Being successful at singleness is about owning it, embracing it. It's about living an incredibly full life. It's knowing you are worthy of love. You are a masterpiece. You are capable of anything. You have the abilities to achieve whatever you want. You are magnificent. You are a child of God, who loves you and only ever wants the best for you. God's apparent 'holding back' with one hand, is his giving with another. He isn't withholding marriage and giving you the second-rate option of singleness. Oh no, dear one, he is handing you the equally amazing, equally awesome, equally fulfilling season of singleness. 'If you, then, though you are evil, know how to give good gifts to your children, how much more will your Father in heaven give good gifts to those who ask him!' (Matt 7:11).

And as much as I know you have heard it before, it deserves repeating – there is a reason you are in the stage of life you are in. And no, it's not because you need to 'level-up' to be married or that there is something wrong with you that needs fixing before you're ready to get married. We are *all* broken. We are *all* not worthy of marriage. If we all had to wait until we were 'fixed' or 'better', then no one would be married. You are not half a person. You are a whole human being. Which means this season of singleness is very specific, very direct, very intentional. You are not in it by accident. There is a purpose, and the beauty of this is that we are completely able to seek out God's purpose for this season without having to worry about the needs and wants of another person.

There is purpose to our singleness

I first sat down to write this book mid-2018. I felt drawn to it like a moth to a flame. I couldn't quite get the idea that we needed to change the way we viewed singleness – the way *I* had viewed singleness – out of my head. I put pen to paper (okay, keyboard to screen) and set to work figuring out what singleness was really all about.

I got about 6,000 words in, and then up popped a potential relationship on my radar. And I got distracted. I put the idea down. I stopped writing. I thought that maybe I could pick it up once I had figured out what was up with this new guy – once we were established, maybe. I could write a book on singleness while being in a relationship, right? That's totally credible, right?

Wrong.

I've never been married, so I don't go around giving marriage advice to people. Which is why, realistically, I felt I couldn't write a book on being single while being in a relationship. It was clear that I couldn't even write it on the path of *considering* a transition to relationship.

As you may have guessed, things with me and the new guy didn't work out. I don't think it didn't work out just so I could write a book about being single. But I can see how us not working out may serve God's purposes better. Could I write a book about being single while being in a relationship? Yes. Is it God's best for the message he is trying to communicate? Probably not.

The point is, this season has purpose. Don't lose sight of that. Find the purpose. Find the reason. And by doing so, find success. Find deep connection through your friends and family, and especially your relationship with God. I have found these pursuits to be deeply fulfilling and to bear much fruit.

I fully believe that it's up to the individual to define what success in singleness looks like. What does it look like for you?

FOURTEEN

Challenging Fear

As I have mentioned before, I believe being single is the most opportune time for growth. It's during this season of being single, of dating, of searching that I have found God does some of his best work.

'So, are you married?'

I've lost count of the number of times I have felt a surge of dread in the pit of my stomach when asked this or similar questions. I know full well why the dread surfaces. It's because I don't want to feel ashamed of the answer. 'No, I'm single' still carries so much shame and if I'm honest, it brings up fear as well. The fear of never being able to answer differently because I will end up being single forever.

Emma Watson recently stated she is 'self-partnered',[1] which basically means she isn't actively dating, but she didn't want to use the term 'single'. There is still such stigma around singleness that people are making up their own terminology for how they describe their dating life. I figure if Emma Watson can do it then so can I. I often get asked if I'm putting myself out there enough. I don't really like this term. It feels a little cheap, like I'm a window display begging for people to look at me. Instead, I have decided to refer to my state of singleness as 'actively single', which means I am content in being single but actively seeking the right person to date.

In being 'actively single', I am open and ready for God to bring people onto my radar in his time.

The other day, he brought someone onto my radar, and I felt ready for it. I was at an event with a few of my friends, and once the formalities of the evening were over, we started chatting over cheese and wine. During the course of our conversation we were joined by a guy named Brad, someone all my friends knew but I didn't. It wasn't until we were further into a conversation that I realised Brad had been mentioned to me before as a possible option. As we continued talking, I noticed how easily our conversation flowed.

Before we knew it the room had emptied, and Brad and I were some of the few people left. Given we had talked for so long and the conversation was interesting, I thought he would ask for my number. He didn't. We said out goodbyes, and that was it. I didn't leave feeling completely dejected, because I chose to see it as a sign that there are in fact good Christian guys out there.

A few days later, a mutual friend of both of us messaged me. She commented that it looked like Brad and I were getting on well at the event, and asked if I had given my details to him. I told her that he hadn't asked, so I hadn't offered. After a few messages back and forth about whether or not I wanted her to do a little meddling, I agreed to letting her suss things out on his end. But I didn't want anything to be forced. If he was interested great. If not, that was fine too. I felt chilled about it.

As the afternoon wore on, though, I started to feel a bit of panic rise up inside me as I thought more about the situation. It was a strange mix of worry and frustration: worry over the possibility of being contacted by this guy and frustration at myself that I was worried about a potential date. In a moment of desperation, I asked God to show me what was going on for me.

In true Holy Spirit style, he gently opened my eyes through one question: 'What is the fear?'

That question caught my attention.

What is the fear?

The majority of our negative thoughts – in fact, I would go so far as to say all of our negative thoughts – are deeply rooted in fear. Worry is the symptom of a deeper fear. Frustration is the symptom of a deeper fear. Any negative thought can be traced back to a deeper fear. When the Holy Spirit asked that question, my perspective immediately changed. I knew in that moment that if I could figure out the fear driving this worry then I could bring light to the darkness and change how I was feeling.

I spent some time pondering and realised the following:

I have a fear of getting it wrong again.

I have a fear of having to go through the process of heartbreak and healing again.

I have a fear that God won't deliver on this desire of my heart.

I have a fear that my family won't like who I end up with.

I have a fear that I am not pretty enough.

I have a fear that even if I find someone to be with, he will eventually get bored of me because I am not interesting enough.

This isn't even a comprehensive list; these were just the fears that surfaced as I sat journaling. As I was writing these out, bringing light into the dark places by being honest with myself – not judging the fears, just acknowledging them – I had a moment of deep insight. Without being conscious of it, I had been using these fears to stay safely single.

I fear getting it wrong, so I write someone off for anything that doesn't align with my list. I have a fear of having to go through the process of heartbreak and healing again, so if I'm not in a relationship then I'm spared that drama. I fear God won't deliver on this desire, so sometimes I try to take matters into my own hands and end up making terrible decisions. But I also fear getting it wrong, so at other times I don't do anything at all, shying away from asking for someone's number or showing interest. I fear my family won't like him, so I just don't bring anyone home. I fear I am not attractive, so I friend-zone guys immediately to avoid testing the waters on whether they're interested, saving myself from the hurt. I fear that a guy will eventually get bored of me, so I don't get close enough for the 'real me' to be visible.

I hide behind my fears, using them as a defence. These fears manifest in many ways. They are my checklists. They are my strategies for not getting it wrong. They are my avoidance of unknown territory like the online dating space. They are my complaints that there are no good Christian guys out there. They are my friend-zone tactics. They are my walls, so you don't get to see the real me. They are my moments of anger at God. They are, to some extent, the reason I am single. They are the resistance that keeps me single. They are single me. Despite all my prayers and dreams and fasting and believing and trying to trust God, the reality is that *deep down I am keeping myself single* because of my fears. I'm *choosing* to be safely single.

This realisation was deeply challenging. I could see how my fears, not God, had been contributing to my singleness. It's clear that there is a part of me that has actually wanted to stay single in order to avoid major hurt. But there is another part of me that wants to experience all the highs and lows of marriage. These two sides are often at war with each other. But if there is anything that I have learnt about this wrestle, it's that I don't want fear to get in the way of experiencing all this life has to offer, especially marriage.

How do I get out of this fear-based mindset?

First, I've started accepting the fears for what they are. Change doesn't come by judging or berating myself for my fears. The heartbreaks I have experienced for these fears to be birthed were real, and I need to have grace for myself.

Second, I choose to release the fear. I choose to put it down. I choose to let it go. Even if all I can manage is to put it down for a minute or two, at least I've put it down.

This process of releasing our fears and no longer choosing to be safely single is a long journey. I have found I need to do it over and over again, especially in the moments when the fear is triggered, like those messages with my friend. The moment I feel negative thoughts or feelings arise about a dating scenario, I now immediately ask, 'What fear is this coming from?' I often find the Holy Spirit answers that question pretty quickly, because he does not want me living in fear. Perfect love drives out fear. We need no longer be directed by our fear but guided by our faith.

I bring the fear to the forefront of my mind, and I pray into it with the truth of God. That he loves me. That he never leaves me. That he is always guiding me. That he is always working for my good. Once I have prayed the truth of God into it, I let it go, releasing it to God and refocusing on what God is asking me to do – to be love and light and of service to others. I often say that over and over to myself: 'Be love and light and of service to others'. It refocuses my mind on what is truly important.

So, my dear single friends, are you playing it safely single? How might your fears be driving your experience? What are you focusing on?

FIFTEEN

Realigning Expectations

When I was seventeen, I met Blake. He went to my church and was an actor with a gorgeous smile and blue eyes. Being both a budding thespian and a hopeless romantic already, I was pretty sure I'd found a guy who (at the tender age of seventeen) would *finally* get me. We were passionate about the same thing, so we were sure to connect deeply, right? And to some extent, we did. The banter was strong and fun, and I quickly confided in my best friend at the time, Sarah, that I liked Blake.

We were both in a church youth drama group. Every year at the youth camp, the drama team would perform short skits in line with the camp theme. The year 11 and 12 students would always get the main roles, and 2001 was my year. Opting to do something a bit different that year, we based the skits on the teen TV dramas that were popular at the time.

The play was '2154: Castle Creek High' and I scored the career-defining role of Taylor, the seventeen-year-old good Christian girl who had a boyfriend played by, you guessed it, Blake. It was my perfect role, performing across from my perfect man.

By this stage, my crush on Blake was bordering on full-blown devotion, but I couldn't tell if Blake liked me. It just wasn't clear, and I felt I had waited long enough. I needed to know if ours was a romance of epic proportions. I wouldn't classify myself as a manipulative person, but if I really want something, I can be driven enough to do whatever to get it, and I wanted to know how Blake felt.

One day, a thought dropped into my head.

The previous year, the drama team had performed a similar play where two of the main characters had kissed. In typical teen style, the audience had whistled and whooped at the sight of these two teenagers (who were actually dating in real life) kissing on stage. Given Blake and I were playing characters who are dating, then to really make it believable to the audience we would probably have to kiss at some point. I mean, it made sense and would really enhance the credibility and believability of our onstage relationship. The level of commitment I had for my craft was at an all-time high – or maybe it was my level of commitment to my crush. If you had asked me at the time, I would have sworn till I was blue in the face that it was for the good of the play, and there was no ulterior motive.

I plucked up the courage and floated the idea with Blake. To my absolute surprise, he said yes.

I was dumbfounded that it had worked – I mean, that he was just as committed to the craft as I was (#oscarbound). I was also ecstatic because, to my mind, this confirmed things. He obviously liked me in some way. Why else would he agree to it? I couldn't believe my luck!

Much as I would have liked to, we didn't rehearse the kiss, instead planning to do it on the morning of the performance – to keep things fresh. It wouldn't be a full-blown kiss, just a peck on the lips at the end of the first scene.

The first day of camp rolled around and my sense of anticipation was palpable. This was it. Blake and I were going to have our chaste little peck, he was going to realise he was in love with me, and we were going to end up together in perfect bliss – on and off the stage.

The scene was going perfectly, with not a single line missed or cue forgotten. Then the moment arrived. I casually threw my final line – something profound like 'See you after school' – and leaned in for my life-changing, on-stage, blow-your-mind kiss.

And just like that, it was over. The crowd whistled and whooped of course, and someone yelled, 'Get a room!' (*so* appropriate for a Christian camp). But none of it mattered. The crowd disappeared as I stared into Blake's eyes. I knew it. This confirmed it. Blake now felt what I felt. I was sure of it. Don't underestimate the power of an on-stage peck-kiss.

The rest of the day I was asked by so many people if that was planned. 'Of course!' I would reply. 'We thought it was an important part to the story.' (I know. I am ridiculous.) I relished the attention, and inside I was floating on air because I was sure Blake felt the same. Never mind that the whole day Blake didn't really make any attempt to talk to me. I was certain he was just biding his time until we could be alone.

Later that evening, I would come to discover that Blake did, in fact, have a crush. Just not on me. It turns out he had fallen for my friend Sarah. My grand plan to ignite a romance of blockbuster proportions had not worked at all, and worse still, my leading man had fallen for the supporting actress. This was a box office flop. I was devastated.

As with all things, time passed, my feelings changed, and despite his best efforts to pursue her, Blake and Sarah never dated. She just wasn't interested in him like that.

Driven by expectation

As I reflect on this story and the ridiculousness of my thinking and actions, I am left pondering what drove me to such lengths. Apart from teenage hormones, I can see that a lot of my actions were driven out of desperation. I somehow felt that if I had a boyfriend, then I would have it all. Like the Blake story, there were so many moments in my teenage years where I had made stupid decisions trying to get a guy to like me. All were driven from a heart that was desperate to be loved.

And at the root of the desperation sat my expectations. These expectations were linked to a timeline, a clear sense of how, when and where all this relationship stuff should play out. In my mind, I was going to be married at twenty-two. It just seemed the natural thing. I'm a Christian. We get married young. My mum was married at twenty-two. Therefore, I will be married at twenty-two because I expect to be. I carried these expectations all through my teen years, and they fed my sense of desperation.

Arriving at my twenty-second birthday, I realised that maybe this was not going to be how my story played out. I didn't even have a boyfriend, so my hope of being married at that age went out as quickly as the candles on my cake. *It's okay*, I told myself, *I still have the rest of my twenties*. I would pray fervently that God would not have me single and thirty. That would be a fate worse than death. *Don't be cruel like that, God,* I would implore him. Surely he wouldn't do that to me. So, I adjusted my mental relationship timeline – but not the strength of my expectations, nor the underlying desperation.

And then I entered my thirties, and I realised that my twenties had not played out how I had expected, either. Ask me a few years ago how I was feeling about being single and I might have said I was fine, but in reality I hated it. I might have given the impression I was loving life, but really, I wanted to be loving my husband and starting a family. Once again, my expectations had taken a big hit.

God's holding back unravelled me, because I was forced to hold a mirror up to myself and ask the very confronting question, *Why*? Why do I believe I need to be married in my twenties? Why do I believe I need to have the most amazing career in my twenties? Why do I believe I must have children before I'm thirty? Why do I believe that being single at thirty would be the absolute worst thing that could ever happen to me? Where have these entrenched expectations come from?

Expectations are not foreign to our human condition, but more often than not we are completely unaware of the expectations we hold. We have unspoken expectations about everything. We are constantly guessing at other people's expectations and putting expectations on others – expecting certain behaviours, expecting certain outcomes, expecting this, expecting that.

The Bible tells us to pray expectantly. But praying and believing expectantly isn't about God fulfilling our expectations by answering our prayers and requests exactly as we lay them out. It's about us learning to align our expectations to the will of God. Ultimately, we need to change our expectations.

But it's taken quite a bit for my expectations to shift.

Ahead of me

As a young twenty-something, I naively thought I had to hit all major milestones by a certain age. As all these major milestones have passed me by, God has instead taken me on an inward journey, unravelling the desperation and sense of urgency that was underlying everything. I have come to realise that no matter the age, there is always time.

The challenge for every Christian has always been to remove the expectation that God will behave in accordance with our will instead of the other way around. We place our expectations on God, praying fervently that he will bend to our will and getting disillusioned and bitter when he doesn't do as we ask.

The disconnect lies within the alignment of will. He is the creator God. He is the all-powerful Creator of the universe and for that reason alone, it is our job to seek out and align our will with his. It means we need to lay down our desires, hopes and dreams and believe that the good, good Father we serve will hear those dreams and work them out according to *his* will. A will that is always for us. A will that knows no end to the love it possesses for us. A will that desires to give us good things.

The laying down of our expectations is wrapped up in how well we can seek out and align ourselves to God.

I arrived at thirty very much single – after all, Justin had broken up with me a few weeks before my thirtieth birthday, so when I say I was very much single, I mean it. Soon into this journey of being single in my thirties, I realised there was no point in fighting it. I had hoped and planned and schemed and tried my hardest to find love in my twenties, and it hadn't worked out despite my best efforts, no matter how many times I had prayed 'in your name'. I woke up to a season where I thought I would have a husband and a family and that life, therefore, would be dictated by my family. But I didn't have a husband and I didn't have a family. And in a defining moment, I realised I had this unique freedom to explore what my thirties looked like without being tied to someone. I had the opportunity to live a truly fulfilling life – if I could only set aside my will for the will of God.

In that moment, I laid aside the expectation of being married to a godly man and starting a family within my timeframe and allowed a new thought, a new way of thinking, to fill my mind. Maybe, just maybe, God had a better plan for me. Maybe I might get to experience what it's like to adopt or foster a child. Maybe I won't have kids at all! Maybe I'll marry later in life. Maybe I'll marry a man who has been divorced or widowed. Maybe I'll marry a man who has never had a girlfriend. Who knows!? The possibilities are endless and equally fulfilling. But I couldn't see the possibilities if I didn't allow for my own expectations to be broken down.

I had built walls of expectation up around me, telling God what I expected to happen with my life. What I didn't realise was that my walls of expectations were so high, I couldn't see what God had for me. I couldn't see all the other things just out of my view that were fulfilling and exciting and huge blessings. After removing my expectations, brick by brick, I have found a sense of certainty that God had wonderful plans for me.

What I have learnt, as the Lord has allowed me to age, and in turn added a drop or two of wisdom and insight into my mind, is that if I can remove the expectation without losing the desire or want, then I have a chance of living an amazing, adventurous, fulfilling life. By setting aside my expectations, my will, and seeking out God's will, I can find fulfilment in the now while being able to hold the future in his name, lightly.

I think one of the most exciting things about still being single is (and I really hope you hear me on this): I still have all of the possibilities – marriage, children – *ahead of me*.

Where some of my friends have hit these milestones in their twenties – I am yet to experience them. I have a potential marriage and a family to look forward to. These are unchartered, undiscovered waters for me, sweet seasons of discovery, change and growth yet to be experienced. And in the meantime, I get to live a truly awesome life because I am single. And the reality is, you do too. You have a wonderful adventure ahead of you, both in singleness and in marriage.

By removing the expectations and seeking alignment with God, I have begun to see the joy that resides in being single and have truly come to appreciate this season for what it is. There is actually a lot to be grateful for when I stop and take a look at my life. And that is a powerful and exciting position to be in.

The Beauty of Single Me

SIXTEEN

Freedom

I have a sister, and she is awesome (you're welcome, Mel!). We are pretty close, but we lead very different lives. Mel is married and has two kids. She is an amazing mother. Whenever I call, she will generally have at least one if not both of her daughters with her, driving them to swimming, picking them up from school, dropping one off here, taking the other one there.

One day, while talking on the phone with her, I mentioned some plans I was making for overseas travel. Mel commented, 'Oh gosh – I'd love to do that.'

'Well, why don't you?'

'Because I have children and a husband that I need think about.'

'So, go anyway?' I said, half-jokingly.

'I would love to have travelled as much as you have! But it's not going to happen. At least, not for a little while.'

I realised in that moment that my sister – whom I look up to, whose life I perceive as awesome, who has everything I want – was actually envying *me*. I have been deeply jealous at times of Mel's marriage and her family, but in that moment the tables had turned, and I realised for the first time that there were things about me that she felt she lacked. Well, not me exactly, but my freedom – the freedom I have to travel as I please, whenever I please, not having to consider anyone.

Born free

It's the one thing every married person is envious of when it comes to single people. Our freedom. We have the freedom to do as we please without needing to consider anyone else. We can book spontaneous trips. We can take up opportunities when they present themselves. We can change our mind. We can sleep in. We can spend our money how we choose. We can do a myriad of things that do not require us to check in with anyone else.

Over the years I have loved this freedom – and hated it as well. I hate it in moments where I'm lonely or jealous or feeling rejected. But I love it when I'm standing at the international airport about to fly to America for a five-week trip I decided to go on only three weeks earlier. I love it when I come home to beautiful silence after spending a few hours with my rather large and loud family. I love it when I can say 'Yes!' to last minute drinks with the girls on Friday night.

What I have also come to realise over the years about this freedom is that it is not designed solely for me. I have 'freedom hours', but how I spend them matters. This became clear to me when I read this passage many years ago:

> *I would like you to be free from concern. An unmarried man is concerned about the Lord's affairs – how he can please the Lord. But a married man is concerned about the affairs of this world –*

how he can please his wife – and his interests are divided. An unmarried woman or virgin is concerned about the Lord's affairs: Her aim is to be devoted to the Lord in both body and spirit. But a married woman is concerned about the affairs of this world –how she can please her husband. I am saying this for your own good, not to restrict you, but that you may live in a right way in undivided devotion to the Lord. (1 Cor 7:32–35)

It's passages like this that make me realise I'm a spoiled brat sometimes! Because my first instinct in reading this passage is to assume that being 'concerned with the Lord's affairs' has to be: 1) only about serving at church; and 2) boring. Boring because you have to only think about God. (Okay, I know that pondering the Infinite Creator of the Universe in all of his dynamic and mysterious ways is actually quite wonderful; I'm just not sure I'm cut out for it full time.)

But I have come to realise that this 'concern about the Lord's affairs' is so much more than stepping up my service at church. The Lord's affairs do not reside within four walls. This passage is speaking to the way we spend our 'freedom hours'. I am all for the impromptu travel, sleep-ins and seeing friends whenever we want – but this passage reminds us that our time is not just our own.

Spending those freedom hours

Over a year ago the electricity went out in my apartment block. Living by myself means when things like this happen I'm often left wondering how on earth will I figure out what to do on my own. Unsure whether or not this power outage only affected my apartment, I gingerly poked my head out the door and saw that the hallway lights were on. My mood dropped – perhaps it *was* just my apartment affected. I went back inside and put some shoes on, ready to hunt down the power box and see if a fuse or something had blown. This is one of those downsides to singleness – when you don't have someone to figure out complex situations like fuse boxes with! Lucky God already had a solution waiting for me in the hallway. As I stepped out of my apartment again, the couple from across the hallway were doing the same.

'Is your electricity out?' I asked.

'Yeah, yours?'

'Yes!' I replied, elated.

The three of us trudged down to the electricity box and flicked on and off every switch we could find. Nothing changed. After we had spent twenty minutes doing pretending to know what we were doing, we called it quits, let the building manager know and decided to wait for the power to come back on. By this time, the neighbours and I were on first-name terms, and the woman, Ange, and I had exchanged numbers. Ange insisted that I let her know if I needed anything. She had extra candles, extra food, and should I need company, I was welcome any time. For this single gal, it was sweet to be welcomed so generously.

Unfortunately, the power was out for thirty-six hours. Fortunately, I made a great friend out of it. We now regularly meet up for coffee and walks. Ange will often make me dinner and drop it over, and we've been able to support each other. What I enjoy most about being friends with Ange, though, is offering my freedom. Ange has two little humans under her care, so her time is rarely her own. I can see, at times, the weariness she feels when she has been up for the fourth night straight with a crying baby or has had to keep the kids cooped up inside all day because it's raining, while I've been able to get a full eight hours sleep or stay snuggled under the covers, reading. I love being able to take one of the greatest benefits of my singleness – my freedom – and lend it to someone who doesn't have it. Sometimes I'll offer to look after the kids for an hour or so just so Ange can go for a run or duck up to the shops or sleep if she needs to. I have many of these 'free hours' to myself, and one of the ways I enjoy spending them is by gifting them to someone who doesn't have the luxury I have.

To me, *this* is being concerned with the Lord's affairs. And it is rarely boring.

Our freedom is one of the greatest gifts we have to offer the world. We have the freedom to be able to drop everything at a moment's notice to be there for a friend or family member when they need us to be. Our freedom allows us to serve others. Our freedom allows us to fill the roster gaps at church. Our freedom is not just a blessing for us, but a blessing to those around us.

How unique and special this is! It is special because the expectation and reality, once you're married, is that you will not have this freedom again. You'll be the one looking to your single friends, asking to borrow an hour of their freedom, remembering what it was like to leave the house without checking in first or sleeping through the night without a child's foot in your face.

Once we say, 'I do', we surrender our freedom hours. We won't get this time back. Our time, our home, our bed will no longer be our own. Sure, we will forfeit freedom hours for something great (or so I'm told). Until that moment comes, love the freedom you have.

SEVENTEEN

Contentment

Back in 2016 I purchased a business with some friends. I didn't realise it at the time, but it would be one of the most defining decisions of my life. Not because the business has taken off and I'm rolling in my millions, but because of the exact opposite. This business has required huge sacrifices on my part, one of which was the releasing of a very comfortable salary from a secure job.

In a single decision, I cut my annual salary to a third and increased my sweat equity by about a billion percent. It was not an easy trade, and it has not been an easy journey. But then again, no growth opportunity is ever easy. One of the things I have come to understand through this journey is that, if it feels like it's all too hard or too much or like nothing is happening, more often than not, what I really need is to look at things from a different angle. Perspective is everything.

This approach to my business has really rubbed off on the way I think about singleness. I am now a firm believer that we have the power to make singleness something worth loving just by the way we think about it and the value we ascribe to it. Is the glass half full or half empty? It all depends on how we look at it.

> *I am not saying this because I am in need, for I have learnt to be content whatever the circumstances. I know what it is to be in need, and I know what it is to have plenty. I have learnt the secret of being content in any and every situation, whether well fed or hungry, whether living in plenty or in want.*
> *(Phil 4:11–12).*

Perspective. I believe it is the 'secret sauce' to Paul's comment in Philippians, where he tells us he has learnt to be content in everything, with anything. Now as we all know, Paul was single, and he is often held up as the ultimate example of the single Christian life. In my view, there's quite a difference between being 'called' to singleness, like Paul, and learning to live with, and love, the journey of singleness without a clear calling. Paul is the exception and not the rule when it comes to modelling the single life. That said, Paul gives a key lesson to all of us who are on the singleness journey. The lesson is this: it's all in how you look at it. Paul could look at either plenty or lack and be content in it. He could see within his lack the plenty that existed. Likewise, he could have a well-fed belly, remember the pain of hunger and be grateful for his current plenty.

I sometimes think about this when I look at the night sky. Light and dark co-exist, but we can't fully appreciate one without the other. We can only see the darkness of night against the contrast of the light of the moon. It's all about which one you give your attention to.

When it comes to learning to love this path of singleness, it really does come down to perspective. Is the glass always half full or half empty? Here are some of the ways that I've challenged my own view of things and found a fresh perspective.

I may not have a spouse, but I have strong, non-romantic relationships

Let me say it again – we're wired for connection (Brené Brown). We need each other. We need people in our lives. But this isn't just about having a large network of people around you (I can hear the introverts' heart palpitations from here!). It is about quality over quantity. When you're single, you have more time to build the quality into your friendships.

I have been able to forge a deep connection in a number of friend-ships because I am single. An example is Chris, one of my closest male friends. He is single, too. We don't see each other a lot because we live in different states, but we catch up semi-regularly, checking in on each other, sharing what's going on in our lives and generally cheering each other on. We have known each other for years and years, and I truly value this strong, non-romantic relationship. I used to think these types of friendships weren't as important as finding a husband, but I've come to see that friends like Chris keep me engaged with the beauty that can be found in life right now.

When I feel lonely, I have a few really good friends I know I can reach out to and be real with. You may have heard of the study that found that loneliness has the same mortality impact as smoking fifteen cigarettes a day. But another similar study found that perceived loneliness – feeling alone even when in a relationship – has the same potential mortality impact as actual loneliness. At least when I'm feeling lonely, I can find someone I actually want to be around to spend some time with, rather than being tethered to a situ-ation where I feel lonely even when I am with someone.

I may sleep alone, but I sleep better (and longer!)

Tell me you haven't felt a little bubble of joy when you've crawled into bed, knowing you get the whole thing to yourself and a night of peaceful, uninterrupted sleep, especially after a long day. My Dad snores like a freight train (sorry Gary, but you do) and as much as I love him, I am *so* glad I am not my mother, who has to sleep next to that noise every night. She has become used to it, which I have huge respect for, but I'm grateful I don't have to put up with something like that. This doesn't mean I'm not willing to get used it – I'm just celebrating that right now I don't have to!

This is one of the benefits of being single that I really enjoy. I'm able to stretch out, snuggle under and sleep for as long as I like, as much as I like, in a bed I have all to myself.

I may only have work to focus on, but I am more successful because of it

Those of us who don't have a family to tend to are often more able to find meaning in our work and pivot our careers when we so desire. We don't have to factor in a significant other when making career choices or worry about who's going to pick up the kids if we need to work back late or opt to go for drinks with the team. We can jump at incredible opportunities like taking up positions overseas or entering the start-up world.

When I decided to take the leap and purchase Thread Harvest back in 2016, I took time to talk to friends and family about the decision. I spent time in prayer, really wanting to know if this was the right next step. The opinion that mattered to me most outside of my own was God's opinion. When I felt a 'Yes' from him, I jumped in, willing to take the risk. It has been one of the most challenging but growth-filled times of my life, and I'm not sure I would have taken the leap if I had a spouse or children to think about. I have learnt so much over this time, and it is taking me in directions I never thought possible (including writing this book!). I can't deny that singleness, while being really difficult at times, has had a positive impact on my career.

I may only have myself, but I know who I am

This is one of my favourite perks of singleness.

I used to think that I had to reach some sort of mythical stage of growth before I was ready to be with someone. Anyone been told that before? When you're 'ready' they will appear? I always wondered what ready was, what it looked like, because I knew plenty of people who clearly weren't all sorted out and somehow managed to find someone.

Then I realised, there's no such thing as 'ready'. We're never ready, because our whole lives are a constant pursuit of becoming more like Christ. This means we will never be the perfect version of ourselves to fully enter into a perfect relationship. We're all broken, and so are our relationships.

When I realised this, I felt a huge weight lift off my shoulders because it was no longer about becoming something and then finding someone. It became about:

   1. Acknowledging I'm broken.

   2. Developing a greater level of self-awareness.

   3. Finding the help I need to become a better version of myself.

I see many people around me having to figure out who they are because they were married so young. I see many people getting a divorce because what they were told they should want in their twenties is not what they actually want. Maturing into self-awareness is something we all have to do, but some ways of doing it are more painful than others. When I look at it, I think growth through singleness is a sweet way to go.

I may eat alone more often, but I'm healthier for it

When I started to date Justin, I was in great shape, the healthiest and strongest I had ever been. But as soon as we started dating, it became harder and harder to get to the gym. I wanted to spend time with him rather than working out. I wanted to cook him yummy, decadent meals instead of sticking to the rabbit food I had been eating before I met him. I wanted lazy weekends with him instead of going to the gym. It wasn't long until I had put back on about 10kg.

After we had broken up and my usual period of emotional eating was over, I began the task of getting back to a healthy version of myself. The intentional time of exercise, meditation, and closeness with God made me healthy again, not only physically but emotion-ally, spiritually and mentally.

Studies have shown that single people are generally healthier than our married counterparts. I really love this part about being single – the freedom to be able to work on myself on my terms, without needing to accommodate someone else's dietary requirements or exercise preferences. I am able to focus on what my body needs. This doesn't mean I'm not willing to accommodate needs of someone else when the time comes; it just means that right now, I can fully focus on looking after myself.

I may get tired of 'being the strong one', but I am more resilient

I watched my nieces and nephews run rampant through the park on an incredibly windy day, desperately trying to hold onto the kite as it flapped around in the air. At some points, this small, flimsy object of fabric, sticks and string looked almost to be pulling the younger ones along, and the kids had to dig deep to hold their ground and hang onto the rebel kite. Other times it dipped and spun and rose, playing with the resistance the wind created. And occasionally, the kite would lose resistance and fall to the ground, at which point, the current kite-wielder would trudge over, pick it up and send it flying into the wind again.

As I pondered the scene before me, I realised I'm like that kite.

The kite would not be able to fly so high, and so consistently, were it not for the wind pushing it. Elevation is only possible when the wind is ploughing into the kite, creating pressure. A resilient kite soars higher and higher, using the wind to propel it forward. In this imagery, I can see the many times I have felt the pressure of singleness, from others' and my own expectations, buffeting against me. At each moment, I can choose to let the pressure keep me on the ground, not wanting to fly again, or I can use it to propel me towards heaven, knowing that it's strengthening me.

Next, when a kite is really in its element, it dips and spins and soars with the wind, almost playing with it, enjoying the way the wind pushes it to go higher and higher. In the same way, I have felt most in my element when I have been able to identify the pressure against my wings for what it is – an opportunity for growth. A chance to change and soar higher. The more I have called myself out on the things that trigger me in my singleness, the greater ability I have to rise above them.

Finally, the kite needs a great handler. A good kite flyer shows deep commitment to their task. They don't let the kite fly off entirely, no matter how hard it fights. They give the kite enough string to soar and fly, but they act as an anchor, tethering the kite to the ground so it can't veer off course into trees or powerlines. And when the kite inevitably dives to ground, having lost the push of the wind, the kiteholder lovingly picks it up, dusts it off, checks it over and launches it back into the sky again.

Is this not the image of God? He allows us to know the pain of pressure to enable the dizzying heights of growth and joy. He frees us to soar but won't let us go. He keeps us tethered to him so that we don't end up in a tree or powerlines. And when we fail, as we inevitably will, he lovingly walks over, picks us up, dusts us off and sends us up into the sky again to be strengthened.

Recently, I was talking to a friend about a piece I've been writing with the underlying message, 'Single girl, you are strong'. When I shared this with her, she rolled her eyes and said, 'I'm tired of being strong'. I could understand the sentiment and don't blame her for feeling tired of being the strong one. Sometimes, being strong is tiring. But resilience is created when we allow ourselves to be picked back up, dusted off and released again into the air. As we go on the journey with God, we build resilience that spills over into all areas of our lives.

How we see anything is how we see everything. There is a lot that is hard about singleness, but by looking for the positives in light of the negatives, we can change our experience. There will always be pros and cons to singleness, seasons of plenty and seasons of lack. Contentment can be found in both, if we are willing to shift perspective.

Is the glass half full or half empty?

EIGHTEEN

Gratitude

I sat in my bed as I do every morning, sipping on a coffee and pondering why I was feeling so flat. I had hoped my flat mood from the day before would be gone when I awoke, but sadly it had sat waiting for me, greeting me with full force when I opened my eyes. I was frustrated it hadn't lifted, which only made matters worse. My flat mood was coming from yet another wave of loneliness, yet another round of 'what if' and 'if only', and I was tired not only of the feelings but of the pattern.

Trying to break the negative spiral, I decided to ask myself some questions to see if I could figure out the root cause of my feelings. Maybe once I had discovered what it was, then I could remove it and feel better again.

I began with 'why'. Why was I feeling this way?

Because I feel lonely. I feel like I'm never going to find anyone. I feel like it's too hard the older I get because the pool of guys gets smaller. I feel like it will never happen.

What is it that I want?

I want a husband and family.

'It can't just be that though…' I reasoned with myself. What is it about having a husband that I want?

I want to feel love and give love.

'Is that all?' I asked myself. What exactly did I want from obtaining my desire?

I took a minute to visualise what I wanted. I let my imagination take me to the first image that came to mind. I could see myself sitting on a couch with my husband. We were laughing because the kids had put on a show or said something funny. The room looked cosy and warm and full of love and laughter. It made me smile.

I paused the scene in my head, wanting to observe what it was about this image that I wanted so much. I noticed how happy I looked and wondered what I would be feeling in that moment if it were true. Peace, contentment, love, joy and balance were the five things that came to mind – the exact opposite of what I was feeling in the present.

Then I had one of those moments where you relearn something you kind-of-already know but have somehow forgotten. I realised that none of those things were exclusive to that scene. Every single one of those emotions were available to me *right now*. I didn't have to wait for a husband or a family to feel them.

That revelation changed my whole perspective. The thing I most desired was a feeling state, not a situation. And even though my imagined scenario might evoke them, those emotions I most wanted to feel – peace, contentment, love, joy and balance – did not require a couch with a husband and some kids.

Feeling over circumstance

That's the beautiful thing about emotions. They transcend circumstance.

It strikes me that this is why we desire anything, right? To *feel* a certain way, to experience a desired emotional state. Think about a time when you worked really hard to achieve a goal, win a race, receive an award. I suspect you were motivated by the feelings of elation, joy and pride you knew you would feel when your work paid off. Oh sure, you also got a trophy, a medal or some other form of recognition, but all those things ever did was to serve as a reminder of the moment you felt the joy, elation and pride. In fact, you could throw out the medal or trophy and still feel those things, because the emotion tied to that event transcends the event itself. You don't need to experience it again to know how it felt.

But here's the thing. We don't actually need to receive what we desire in order to feel how we want to feel. We often let our external situation dictate how we feel, but the powerful truth is that we can access the feelings we long for regardless of our situation.

Jesus asleep in the boat is the perfect example of how our emotions do not need to be dictated by our circumstance.

> *Then he got into the boat and his disciples followed him. Suddenly a furious storm came up on the lake, so that the waves swept over the boat. But Jesus was sleeping. The disciples went and woke him, saying, 'Lord, save us! We're going to drown!'*
>
> *He replied, 'You of little faith, why are you so afraid?' Then he got up and rebuked the winds and the waves, and it was completely calm.*
>
> *The men were amazed and asked, 'What kind of man is this? Even the winds and the waves obey him!' (Matt 8:23–27).*

This story highlights the two responses available to us in any given situation. First there are the disciples, frantic and afraid of their circumstances. The wind and waves crashing against the boat, unable to see where they are going, fearful they will lose their lives.

Then there is Jesus, asleep. At total peace and rest. Not worried one little bit about his external circumstances. I would love to feel so at peace in such turbulent circumstances, to feel that despite all that is raging around me and all that I lack (like smooth seas and light to guide me), I am able to remain in peace.

Jesus gets up and calms the storm, asking the disciples why they are so afraid. Once he has calmed the storm, the men return to feelings of peace and calm and a whole lot of awe at Jesus. But those feelings were available to them even in the midst of the storm. That's what Jesus shows us in this. They, too, could have had peace and rest, but they focused on what was around them and let that determine their feelings.

It's all available to you now

The thing about being single is that what you desire to feel is actually available to you now. You can feel the love you seek. You can feel the joy you want. You can feel the contentment you desire. All of what you want is available to you now through Jesus. That may feel a little bit like a Sunday School answer for some people, but just because it sounds simplistic doesn't mean it's not useful and worth putting to the test.

Let me be honest – I've found this a difficult truth to enter into. I think this is because so much of being single is about waiting for something to happen: waiting for a potential date, a potential spouse, a new life. In the waiting, a tiny part of me has worried that if I feel good *now* – feel joy, feel love – perhaps God will leave me where I am. As if feeling at peace in my current situation means 'giving up' on hope for a relationship in the future.

But we don't need to be devoid of what we're really seeking while in the waiting. The disciples didn't need to wait for the storm to be calmed to feel the peace that Jesus felt, and we don't need to wait for a romantic relationship to feel the love we want. Because let's face it, that is what we really want. We want love.

Cultivating gratitude

When I find myself forgetting this truth, as I do regularly, I turn to the practice of gratitude. Shifting to an attitude of gratitude is the doorway to feeling how you want to feel. When we're grateful, we're able to see things differently.

I first started this practice in the aftermath of the break-up with Justin. Knowing that I was in a deep funk and would need to be proactive about shifting my mindset, I took part in a 'Thirty Days of Grateful' challenge on social media. Each day, I posted a picture about one thing that I was grateful for that day.

My first post was a picture of a candle and droplets on my shower door with the caption, 'Today I am grateful for pretty candles and hot showers… they soothe a weary soul'. The next day it was a picture of a dear friend of mine who had blessed me with cups of tea and a listening ear. The third was about two songs that were helping me through this tough time and some flowers a friend had given me. And so it went, every day, for thirty days, finishing on my thirtieth birthday with a photo of a Pandora bracelet I had received from my family and the following caption: 'I have spent the last thirty days being grateful every day for at least one thing. From friendship, to spontaneous moments, to family, to the smallest of things. But as I land here on day thirty, which is also the day I turn thirty, I am truly grateful for one thing – the cross. Without it, the last thirty days, the last thirty years and the years to come are pointless. My God is an awesome God.'

Our thoughts are so powerful. I went from only being able to be grateful for a candle to feeling gratitude for everything God had done in my life. It was a long journey to get there, but I was able to change my mind, my thoughts, little by little, which in turn changed my perspective and healed my heart, little by little. Having an attitude of gratitude doesn't leave much space for bitterness to grow. It will remove your view that you have been forgotten. It will very quickly put out the fire of jealousy. It lifts your heart and mind out of sadness. It reminds you that you are not alone. It will help you have grace for those who don't understand.

Gratitude works much like a muscle. The more you work it, the stronger it becomes. And just like muscles help us move better, gratitude helps us see better. Gratitude helps me ascribe value to myself in this moment and to this season. It also helps me see how God is active in this journey with me. 'Praise the Lord. Give thanks to the Lord, for he is good; his love endures forever' (Ps 106:1).

Gratitude especially helps me to tap into the truth that what I most seek is already available to me. I start to see all the love that exists in my life already. I have a family who deeply love me. They include me in their lives, involve me as an equal and welcome me as I am, with or without a spouse. I have friends who love me, who check in on me regularly and cheer me on, who will sit in the dirt and dust with me or and join me for a last-minute wine at the rooftop bar down the street.

And then there's God. God IS love. And he is constant, never-changing, always present.

When we are willing to look for it, we can notice that we are already surrounded by love. It may not be the romantic love we wish for, but my gosh, we are loved more than we will ever realise. My dear single friend, how cool is it that the thing we are looking for was here all along. Now that's a *Selah* moment.

NINETEEN

Endurance

The fruits of singleness that I've covered so far – freedom, contentment, gratitude – all sound pretty sweet. But no book on singleness would be complete without addressing one of the less sexy fruits of the single season: endurance. Being single is an endurance sport. It feels great to know I can go a really long distance, but let's face it, the training I've put in has been an absolute killer.

Most of this endurance training comes in a particular form: learning the art of waiting. As human beings we are constrained by the reality of time and as such, waiting forms a natural part of our everyday life. We're always waiting for something – for the barista to make our coffee, our friend to message us back about plans for the weekend, the mechanic to be done with our car. There's always something to be waiting for. Short wait times are easy. It's the long, drawn out wait that seems to be the hardest, especially when you're not sure if God is at work.

I'll be honest. I'm built for the sprint, not the marathon. I have desires and dreams for my life, things I want to experience, see and explore. I want to make a beeline for them, get them done. Of course, like most Christians, I want to follow the will of God, to be in tune with his will and ensure I'm on the path he has for me. But I also want to achieve my goals and dreams a bit more quickly, please! It's my sense, however, that God cares infinitely more about the journey to the destination than the destination itself. Unfortunately, I operate the other way and usually care more about the destination.

Given this, I've found taking on a long-range view, an endurance mentality, one of the toughest aspects of my faith. Yet, learning to trust God and embrace the waiting seasons he's had me in has led to some of the greatest growth in my faith journey.

Playing the waiting game

Remember my hapless non-relationship with Matt from the 'Forgotten' chapter? You may recall where we left that story: I'd received a text from him saying he was dating someone else. Though I was devastated, I'd responded after a few days, wishing him well. I thought that text was going to be the end of it. Turns out, it wasn't.

In the days after Matt's text, I spent a lot of time seeking God and trying to make sense of it all. In a moment of deeply crying out to God, I felt the Holy Spirit encourage me to wait a year. A year? I'd already invested so much of myself into this, and he wanted me to wait another year?! Reluctantly, I agreed. I was too broken, hurt and confused to argue. I needed to heal, and the only way I knew how to do that was to cease all contact.

I set out to distance myself from Matt and focus on healing not just my broken heart but my broken relationship with God. Given that I'd received what I felt to be a word from God about Matt, my trust in God was well and truly broken, as was my confidence that I knew the voice of God. I didn't feel I could trust myself with any sort of leading from God. Layer into that my shattered self-image and the usual internal barrage of unkind thoughts – too ugly, too needy, too stupid – and I became more and more broken. I felt like a small bird that had been hit by a Mack truck and was trying to heal itself.

The process was long and complicated. I wanted to run from God because I felt he had hurt me, but I needed him because I was so hurt. I couldn't understand why after such constant affirmation I could find myself in deep heartbreak. What made matters even more difficult was this sense in my spirit that somehow God was not done yet. I didn't know exactly what to do, only that I knew I needed to wait and focus on healing.

Matt was never far away, often reaching out via a like on Facebook or Instagram, random smiley face messages and that kind of thing – small attempts to mend the connection. I ignored every one of them. I had decided that if Matt didn't want me, then I'd show him what he'd rejected. So, I threw myself into the gym junkie life (haven't we all at some point after a heartbreak?) and was feeling clearer of mind, stronger both mentally and physically. And I began edging my way back to trusting God, because in it all, he felt like the only constant.

I eventually broke my freeze-out with Matt and responded to a message, reasoning that we had gotten on so well – why couldn't we at least have some sort of friendship? As I did this, I felt my old feelings resurface, and the more I continued down this path, the more I felt like I was supposed to wait. I don't know what I was expecting to happen; I simply felt that God was telling me to wait. I gave God till the end of May for something to change. May arrived and nothing was different. Matt was still with his girlfriend, still in contact with me every now and then, and I was still being strung along.

That was it. I pulled the plug. No more Matt. I deserved better. If God was as all-powerful as he said he was, then if he really wanted

Matt and I together he could make it happen, but I was done waiting. So, I gave it over that day and looked to moving forward.

Waiting in good company

This may sound like a negative story of waiting – and giving up on waiting. I was focused on a particular 'destination' – Matt. Turns out, God had me waiting for a different reason altogether. He was much more interested in my journey.

Through my season of waiting – for Matt, for resolution, for God's clear answers – I learnt something new. Waiting is hard. That's not the new bit. Everyone can agree with that. Holding onto the hope that God is moving even when I can't see him doing anything is hard. When our experience of reality doesn't match the hope in our hearts, it's painful. When we're waiting for a desire to be fulfilled, everything we're feeling gets amplified. It's hard to see other people get what we desire. It's hard to not become disillusioned or bitter. It's hard not to lose focus and give up. It's hard not to walk away and settle for something less than ideal.

But waiting is also refining.

Waiting is the act of staying in place or delaying action until a certain time or event. It is standing still and doing nothing. This is something we, as single people, are told not to do. We are encouraged to be active in getting out there and meeting new people, taking initiative to change our situations. But could there be more to waiting than we have been led to believe? Is waiting simply inaction, or is the act of waiting putting us right where God wants us?

I found during the time I was 'waiting for Matt' that my relationship with God went through a baptism of fire. It was burnt to the ground and built back up. When I think about the time I spent waiting for

Matt, what I was really doing was abiding in Jesus. That whole experience has been one of the defining faith moments of my life.

Waiting is not meant to be a season of passivity or killing time. As we see modelled for us in the Bible, waiting serves a faith-building purpose. It is in the very nature of standing still that the we really experience the powerful refinement waiting has to offer.

I found the following quote one day:

Noah waited 120 years.

Abraham waited 25 years. Jacob waited 20 years.

Joseph waited 13 years. Moses waited 40 years. David waited 12 years Jesus waited 30 years.

If God is making you wait, you're in good company.

Waiting is part of our walk with God. It truly is a discipline. It teaches us to focus on God's will, not our own, and it reminds us of the power of God. He won't lead us somewhere that we're not ready to go.

It's tough to write that, because from my perspective I'm so ready to be married. I was ready when I met Matt, I was ready when I met Justin, and I've been ready every day since. But I can't help wondering what God's view might be.

One of the most fascinating waiting stories in the Bible is Moses. Moses waited forty years, wandered the desert for forty years, had to look after a whingy bunch of Israelites for forty years and then didn't even get to see what he was waiting for – the Promised Land. Moses never received what he was waiting for. Yet, he is counted as one of the greatest men of the Bible, favoured by God.

I can hear Moses now: 'You had me wander all these years, taking care of a disgruntled group of people, and *I'm* not allowed to enter the Promised Land?!'

I think we can learn a lot from Moses about waiting well. He didn't get to enter the Promised Land, but he did get to do some pretty cool things. Moses experienced firsthand the grace and kindness of God when he watched manna fall from the sky. He hit a rock with a stick and water flowed. He saw the power of the love of God in the form of a pillar of smoke by day and a pillar of fire by night as God led his people. He saw seas turned into dry land. And one of the most incredible things Moses experienced was seeing the back of God pass him by. All of that because he waited.

What could we be missing in the waiting?

In waiting for Matt, I experienced things in my walk with God I may never have known otherwise. The nights where I felt the very presence of God around me as I cried over whether or not I should keep waiting for Matt. The powerful way God drew my attention to the Bible passages that kept me going. The loving support of friends, who came alongside me and did not judge me for believing that God had given me a word.

Yes, singleness is a test of endurance, but it's one I'm willing to give myself over to now. In reality, I could easily jump online or head out on the weekend and find someone to be in a relationship with. But my preference, my heart's preference, is to wait for God to bring a good man in at the right time. I look back over those who have had to wait for their heart's desires, like those men of faith in the Bible, and I figure if God is asking me to wait, then I'm in good company.

TWENTY

Surrender

The singleness season can only be fruitful when it is accompanied by a fully surrendered heart. When everything is stripped away, what we're left with is a journey of waiting and a choice of surrender.

If I had to summarise the message of this book into one sentence it would be this – learn to truly surrender while you wait, because any other option will leave you angry, broken and questioning a loving God who *does* have a plan for this area of your life.

That's it. Surrender is the whole game.

Surrender is what God is constantly inviting us into. He does not control us, but he is constantly leading us to a point of surrender to his will. Not only because his ways are better than ours but because it's in surrender we find peace. It's in surrender we find guidance. It's in surrender we find joy and love. It's in surrender we find growth. It's in surrender we find ourselves. And he wants us to know those things, as any good, loving Father would.

The structure of this book is not an accident. As I mentioned at the start, I didn't want to provide advice on how to get out of being single. Instead, I wanted to provide insights and lessons from my own experiences in the hope you would feel less alone, be encouraged in your singleness and perhaps arrive at a point where you can fully embrace it – even love it. Each story I've shared, each 'aha moment', has ultimately led me to the realisation that surrender is the whole game. I thought I knew it, but my experience shows me – and you – that I didn't. Not really. Not how God wants me to know surrender.

Singleness holds lots of challenges. Perhaps the greatest of these is our inability to truly let go.

Many of us let things go for a time and then pick them up again. I did this over and over again. And can I let you in on a secret? It's really tiring trying to strong-arm God into doing your will. The energy you exert fighting so hard for something is not worth it, especially when what you're fighting against is actually better than what you could ever hope or imagine.

Believing that, and surrendering to it, is no easy task. God's 'better' may mean being single for the rest of your life. I know. Even writing that makes me feel anxious, because I want to be married. But if the Creator of the universe, who sent his Son to die for me and knows me better than I know myself, were to ask it of me, could I really refuse?

Whatever God might be asking, the truth I have come to know so deeply is that there is no better way to walk the waiting journey of singleness than in true, deep surrender.

Dreams versus expectations

I'm still working this whole singleness gig out. I'm figuring out how to walk in surrender while honouring the desire for a husband and the joy of singleness with equal measure. In this moment, being single is awesome, and I feel gratitude and peace within every fibre of my body as I embrace the world of possibilities before me.

The reason I can embrace it so openly and willingly is because of a deep trust that I am loved more than I'll ever know and a heart fully surrendered to that love. In that surrender, I can give over my dreams so that they remain dreams and not expectations. Our hopes for marriage and a family are not wrong. God has given us the ability to dream, and those dreams, the one's that cause a little smile to form at the corner of your mouth, are beautiful and should be embraced and savoured.

Dreams, hopes and desires are designed to build within us faith and trust. They are requests that we present to God and then release to him, trusting that when God says that he wants to hear about desires because they matter to him, they really do, and having faith in his all-knowing power that if he hasn't released these desires into our lives yet, there's a really good reason for it.

The way dreams can harden into expectations is so subtle. It starts with the desire and moves into a request we present to God. The change, as I have experienced, comes when, while presenting the request, we don't surrender it at the same time. The Bible says to 'present your requests to God. And the peace of God, which transcends all understanding, will guard your hearts and your minds in Christ Jesus' (Phil 4:6–7). It doesn't say, 'Present your requests to God and expect him to deliver on them exactly how you laid them out to him'.

Our desires and dreams aren't meant to become the expectation or standards by which we measure if God remembers or cares for us. Our dreams need to build up our belief that God is good and always working for our good, not lock him down to unfold things in our time or our way. We are to present God with requests, not demands.

And that is where surrender comes in and the peace that transcends understanding is found. Presenting our requests to God *means* surrendering them to his sovereign understanding and plan for our lives.

Surrender is only possible when we trust the One we're surrendering to. It is a daily, sometimes hourly, choice, and it's hard. But I have experienced the true peace that lies on the other side of surrender, and I've come to discover it's worth the internal battle to surrender my will. The way my singleness looks when I am observing it from a place of peace and trust and surrender is far more beautiful, lovely, purposeful and wonderful than I could have imagined.

Surrendering to God

Surrender is not new to the people of God.

I believe it was the only way Esther made it through months of waiting while preparing for her one night with the king. All those days and nights of anticipating, planning, preparing for something that could very well have resulted in heartbreak, rejection and loneliness. Her journey was high stakes. She risked the king having his way with her, rendering her unable to be married to someone else if he then rejected her. She risked saying or doing something that the king might not like, seeing her exiled like her predecessor, Queen Vashti. Esther risked a lot on her journey of love, but she courageously put one foot in front of the other, believing that no matter the outcome, her God had a plan.

I'm sure there were nights where Esther lay awake, feeling the sting of loneliness, being kept away from her family and all that was familiar. I'm sure she feared being rejected, as very few understood what it was like to be in the position she was in. I'm sure she battled jealous attacks from the other women, given she had such great favour with Hegai. She may even have encountered the sting of jealousy herself, derived from a belief that she might not be enough. The pressure of having to do whatever was needed to please the king, the hours, days and months of waiting – these would have had their torturous moments.

Can you imagine living twelve months with a bunch of single women, vying for the attention of one man? I guess you can – it sounds like Esther might have been part of the very first series of *The Bachelor*.

The competition she encountered and the internal battles against fear and loneliness could have been enough to see her give up. Instead, we see a woman who followed wise counsel and embraced the waiting season she was in. She lived it fully, surrendering to God and finding favour with those around her.

This period of time spans only a few passages in the Bible, but it speaks volumes of a single woman embracing where God was leading, trusting his love and his plan for her and living her life fully in the season she's in. There were no guarantees for Esther. She had received no sign from God, no promise, no word that Xerxes would definitely choose her in the end. All she had was her faith that enabled her to trust in a good God who knew the plan he had for her – and ultimately, for his people.

Surrendering to Single Me

As you've surely figured out, having travelled with me throughout this book, I've struggled with living in the present. I often find that I am looking to what's ahead or berating myself for what has been rather than just being with what is. I have lived much of my life believing that my great adventure would begin when I found my husband. I just needed him, and then 'real life' would start.

As the stories in this book show, God has persisted in challenging this belief. Together, we have chipped away at it, removing stone by stone of a belief foundation that was not laid in truth. My life doesn't start when I find my husband. My life is right now, in this moment. I have surrendered my dreams of marriage to an infinitely creative God who knows me better and knows where he is taking me.

I won't lie. I worry sometimes his plan means I won't get married until I'm much older. That I will have to give up on the idea of having children from my body altogether. I allow myself time and the grace to mourn things that didn't turn out the way that I hoped. But I choose to not stay there and instead direct my energy towards believing God knows what he is doing. By acknowledging my finiteness and realising I only have this moment right now, I release and surrender to the Infinite One.

Surrendering to Single You

Surrendering to singleness, to single you, will require a decision on your part. Will you surrender to a Divine Creator? Or will you continue to push against his plan?

My hope and prayer is that you would know the peace that is found in surrender. The wholeness that is found in surrender. The joy that is found in surrender. The deep love of God that is found in surrender. Your worth is not defined by how many relationships you have had or how well they went. Your worth is defined by what Jesus did on the cross.

We can change how we embrace this season. We can change the value we ascribe to singleness. We can change the value we ascribe to those who are divorced, to those who are widowed, to those who are not married and to those who remain celibate. But it starts with us, single person. It starts with you.

'Even if you want to get married, the worst thing you can do is to think of your single state as time-marking,' says Stephanie Coontz, director of research at the Council on Contemporary Families. 'You should enjoy this part of your life, not as a preparatory stage, but as something that is just fun in and of itself.'[1] In other words, your 'real life' doesn't begin when you meet a partner. It's happening right now.

We serve an incredibly creative, dynamic, fiercely loving God who only wants to give us good things. Singleness is a good thing. Living a satisfied single life is possible.

Your real life is happening now. It is in this moment. And you have a choice.

You can choose to replace loneliness with gratitude.

You can choose to release the rejection and embrace yourself.

You can choose to ground yourself in the belief that Jesus would have still gone to the cross just for you.

You can choose to have grace for your moments of jealousy and redirect your eyes to all you do have.

You can choose to enter into a healthy dialogue about sex and be a voice of change.

You can choose to acknowledge waiting is hard but still embrace the waiting and use it for God's glory.

You can choose to step into freedom.

You can choose to step into the character development.

You can choose to shift your attitude to one of gratitude.

You can choose to exercise the wisdom God has given you.

You can choose to change the narrative.

Deeply value your singleness because you are not marking time. This season is filled with incredible purpose. You are called to more than just waiting it out until you get married for your life to start.

You are called to surrender. And in that surrender, you can learn to love singleness. What was once an unwanted path has now become a sacred journey.

Notes

1. You Are Allowed to Feel What You Feel

1. Brené Brown, from her 2010 TEDtalk, 'The power of vulnerability'. Further Brené Brown quotes are from the same source.
2. Carolyn Gregoire, https://www.huffingtonpost.com.au/entry/how-this-harvard-psycholo_us_3727229
3. Dani Treweek, 'The "problem" of singleness', blog post, 8 July, 2018, https://sydneyanglicans.net/blogs/the-problem-with-singleness

3. Rejected

1. Lisa Messenger, *Risk and Resilience: Breaking and Remaking a Brand* (Australia: Messenger Group, 2018).

10. The Idol of Marriage

1. https://sydneyanglicans.net/blogs/the-problem-with-singleness
2. From a sermon by John Macarthur, posted to YouTube April 28, 2016. Quote occurs at 2:32. https://www.youtube.com/watch?v=D7S_zeOxd-g
3. Books written by Marshall Segal, Josh Harris and Elisabeth Elliot, respectively.
4. https://sydneyanglicans.net/blogs/the-problem-with-singleness

11. Just When You Thought You Were Off the Hook, Single One

1. https://sydneyanglicans.net/blogs/the-problem-with-singleness

14. Challenging Fear

1. thesun.co.uk/fabulous/10340864/after-emma-watson-declared-shes-happily-self-partnered-four-women-reveal-why-theyre-single-and-not-dating/

20. Surrender

1. https://www.marieclaire.com/sex-love/advice/a8839/being-single-after-breakup/

Acknowledgements

I can't believe I'm sitting here on Thursday morning typing up my acknowledgements for this book. It has been a long journey. An unexpected journey. But a rewarding one.

This book simply would not have been possible without some very important people in my life making connections, encouraging me to not give up and inspiring me to keep going.

Firstly, to all my friends and family who have asked how my writing was going, encouraged me that this message is important, bought me coffees, let me read and then re-read sections of the book to them, provided feedback and just generally run this race with me, I thank you. I thank you for all the ways seen and unseen you have supported me, loved me and prayed for me as I endeavoured to make this book a reality.

To my parents, Robyn and Gary, I want to say thank you for the prayers, support, proofreading and financial contributions you have made in keeping this book on track. You are an incredible cheer squad, and I am eternally grateful for you.

Kara (Consuela) Martin. I literally would not be writing acknowledgements if it weren't for you. I still vividly remember sitting in our favourite spot at our café and me nervously sharing a vision I had for a book about singleness with you, an established, published author. I have looked up to you from the start. Your generosity, in all its forms, has humbled me, and I will be forever in your debt. Your grace, kindness, connections and general cheering me on has had a profound impact on me. Thank you, from the bottom of my heart. (Please check out her books *Workship: How to Use your Work to Worship God* and *Workship 2: How to flourish at work* at www.workship.com.au)

Beks. What would I do without you? My constant cheerleader, you are always reminding me that my voice matters, my story needs to be shared and, most importantly, to take it one step at a time. Thank you, soul sister. (Please check out her inspiring Enneagram Magazine at www.enneagrammagazine.com and pick up a copy!)

Special mention to Beth Graybill who graciously gave me hours of her time to guide me and encourage me. Thank you for your time and wisdom. Hsu-Ann and Sherene, thank you for reading the very first version and providing your thoughts and feedback, it was incredibly helpful.

Gina Denholm, you saint! This book grew into something better than I could have imagined when I met you. Thank you for holding my story and this book with such care, compassion, grace and wisdom. You are truly a saint for sifting through every word of this book numerous times as you helped me bring it life. I am deeply grateful for your incredible editing skills. I will spend the rest of my life trying to express my gratitude to the depth in which I feel it. Thank you, thank you, thank you!

And finally, no acknowledgement would be complete without thanking the One who has been writing with me and through me from birth. God. You know that none of this was ever my plan but here we are, purely by your grace and wisdom. There are times where I don't like the fact that your plans are better than my own because generally it means that there is going to be some sort refining fire on the journey. But you have shown me over and over again that your plans always, without fail, are better than my own. Single in my thirties was not my plan, but I'm grateful for your kindness in teaching me how to learn to love it. Thank you for gifting me a passion for story and storytelling. I can't wait to see what we will write next…

About the Author

Neri Morris is an inquisitive author and a "figure-it-out-as-you-go" entrepreneur. Story-telling runs through her veins along with a lot of coffee and a love of the ocean. Neri began her writing career in 2020 but has been mastering the art of story since birth. Her first book ***Single Me: Learning to Love the Unwanted Path of Single-ness*** is an insightful, funny and challenging look at singleness in the modern day Christian context.

FORTIFIED is Neri's first fiction novel and is due for release in early 2021. For a free sample excerpt from ***FORTIFIED***, head to nerimorris.com/books

Neri lives on the North Shore of Sydney, Australia. She is the Creative Director of **Thread Harvest** (www.threadharvest.com.au) an ethical online fashion marketplace, an author, speaker and a regular contributor for **Hope 103.2** (www.hope1032.com.au)

To find out more about Neri, head to nerimorris.com or follow her at instagram.com/neri_morris or facebook.com/neri0morris

www.ingramcontent.com/pod-product-compliance
Lightning Source LLC
Chambersburg PA
CBHW070254010526
44107CB00056B/2456